CGP are <u>the</u> KS3 Science experts!

In Year 8, there's a tonne of Science to practise. Luckily for you, this ace CGP Workbook is here to lighten the load, one topic at a time.

Each section has stacks of practice that builds your confidence by starting off easier and getting tougher. There are even plenty of maths and practical questions included to help develop the key skills needed for GCSE Science.

We've also added a mass of test-style practice to make sure everything's sinking in and full answers for every question. I bet you can't weight to start!

CGP — still the best! ☺

Our sole aim here at CGP is to produce the highest quality books — carefully written, immaculately presented and dangerously close to being funny.

Then we work our socks off to get them out to you — at the cheapest possible prices.

Contents

Contents

Published by CGP

Editors: Luke Bennett, Charlotte Burrows, Jack Davies, Katie Fernandez, Daniel Fielding, Paul Jordin, Charles Kitts, Rachel Kordan, Duncan Lindsay, Rachael Rogers, Camilla Sheridan, Charlotte Sheridan and Caroline Thomson.

Contributors: Ian Connor, David Martindill, Kate Reid, Helen Ronan and Jamie Sinclair

With thanks for Emily Smith for the copyright research.

With thanks to Philip Armstrong, Ian Francis, Glenn Rogers, and Jamie Sinclair for the proofreading.

ISBN: 978 1 78908 264 7

Clipart from Corel®
Illustrations by: Sandy Gardner Artist, email sandy@sandygardner.co.uk
Printed by Elanders Ltd, Newcastle upon Tyne.

Based on the classic CGP style created by Richard Parsons.

How To Use This Book

- Place the book on a flat surface ensuring that the text looks like this, not sıɥʇ.
- In case of emergency, press the two halves of the book together firmly in order to close.
- Before attempting to use this book, familiarise yourself with the following safety information:

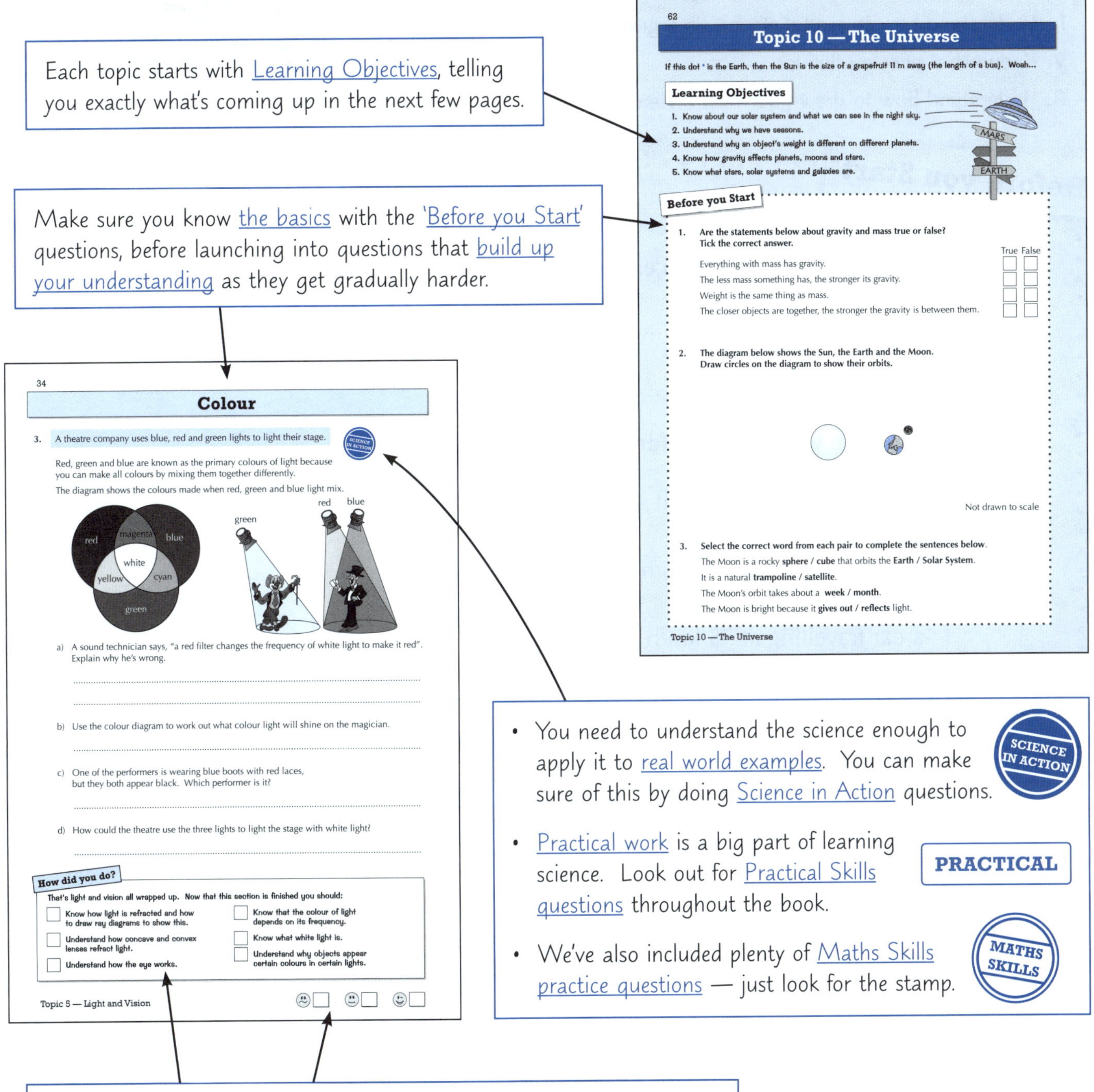

Each topic starts with Learning Objectives, telling you exactly what's coming up in the next few pages.

Make sure you know the basics with the 'Before you Start' questions, before launching into questions that build up your understanding as they get gradually harder.

- You need to understand the science enough to apply it to real world examples. You can make sure of this by doing Science in Action questions. **SCIENCE IN ACTION**
- Practical work is a big part of learning science. Look out for Practical Skills questions throughout the book. **PRACTICAL**
- We've also included plenty of Maths Skills practice questions — just look for the stamp. **MATHS SKILLS**

Use the topic checklist to mark how happy you are with each key point. Then tick the face that matches how you're feeling about the topic as a whole. Keep going back over what you don't know until you do.

Once you've done all the topics, have a go at the Mixed Questions (p.100-104). They'll check you can answer test-style questions on content from the whole book.

You'll find maps online showing where each topic of the AQA Syllabus and the National Curriculum for Key Stage Three Science are covered in this range of Targeted Workbooks. Just head over to: www.cgpbooks.co.uk/ks3scienceresources

Topic 1 — Distance-Time Graphs

These graphs are really just showing how far something has moved in a certain amount of time.

Learning Objectives

1. Understand how to read distance-time graphs.
2. Know what acceleration is.
3. Understand how to draw your own distance-time graphs.

Before you Start

1. Fill in the words in this sentence:

Speed tells you how much .... is travelled in how much ....

2. Which of these will travel the furthest in one hour?

☐ a motorcycle travelling at 48 km/h

☐ a van travelling at 37 km/h

☐ a car travelling at 55 km/h

3. Complete these calculations:

a) A lorry is moving at 30 km/h.
How far will it get in 2 hours? .... km

b) A horse is running at 8 m/s.
How far will it get in 10 seconds? .... m

4. This is a time-distance graph for three runners.

a) Who ran the furthest in 4 minutes?

....

b) Who was going the slowest?

....

distance (m): 0, 200, 400, 600
time (minutes): 0, 1, 2, 3, 4
Rohan
Sue
Austin

Using Distance-Time Graphs

1. The graph shows how far an object has travelled over time.

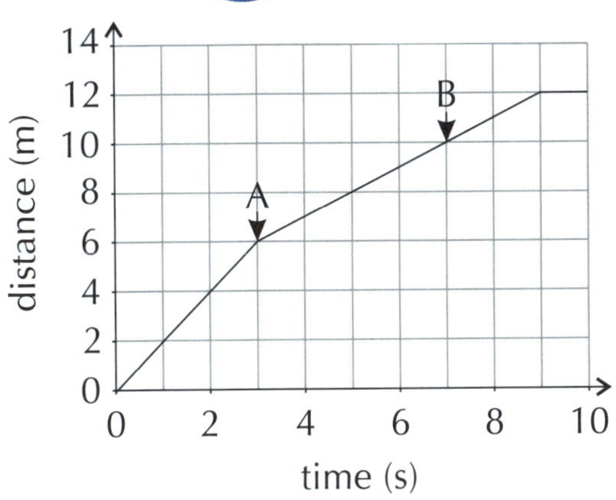

a) How much time has passed at point A?

.... s

b) How far has the object moved at point B?

.... m

c) How long has it taken to travel 12 m?

.... s

2. A train makes journeys back and forth between two stations, Askby and Kirkham. This is a distance-time graph for the train.

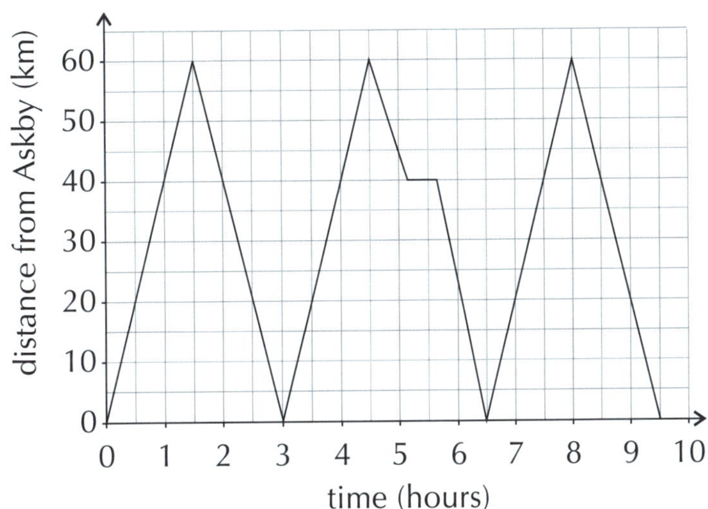

a) How far is Kirkham from Askby? .... km

b) How long does the first journey from Askby to Kirkham take? .... hours

c) The village of Moorgate is located near the railway track, 20 km from Askby. How long after leaving Askby does the train pass Moorgate?

.... hours

d) At one point, the train had to stop because of sheep on the tracks.

i) How far from Askby did this happen? .... km

ii) How many minutes late did the train arrive at the next stop? .... minutes

Using Distance-Time Graphs

3. Describe the distance-time graph for:

a) An object travelling at a constant speed. ....

b) An object accelerating. ....

4. This is a distance-time graph for a tractor.

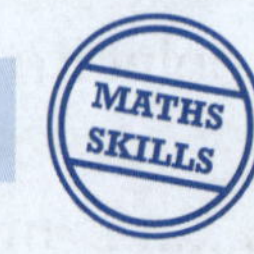

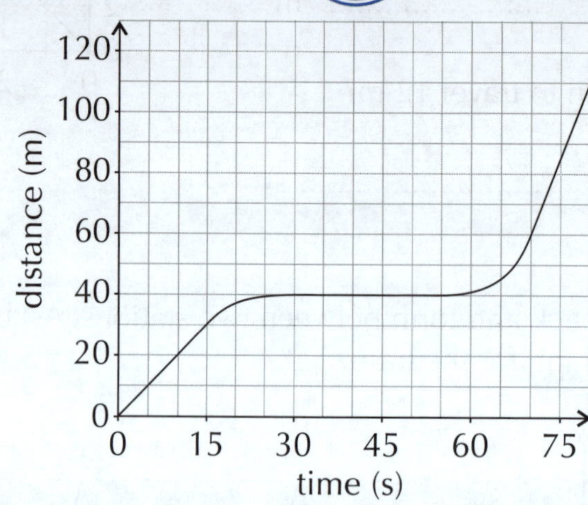

a) What is the speed of the tractor between 0 and 15 seconds?

.... m/s

b) What is happening to the tractor's speed:

i) between 15 and 30 seconds?

....

ii) between 60 and 70 seconds?

....

c) What is the tractor doing between 30 and 55 seconds?

....

d) On a different journey, the tractor sets off at a constant speed, then slows down and stops. Describe what the distance-time graph would look like for this journey.

....

....

....

Drawing Distance-Time Graphs

1. Radha wants to make a distance-time graph to show how her speed changed during a bike ride. She has used a GPS tracker that records her distance from the start every 60 seconds. The table shows the data from the GPS tracker.

Time (s)	0	60	120	180	240	300	360	420	480	540
Distance from start (m)	0	100	200	600	1000	1200	1400	1400	2000	2600

a) Draw a distance-time graph for Radha's bike ride.

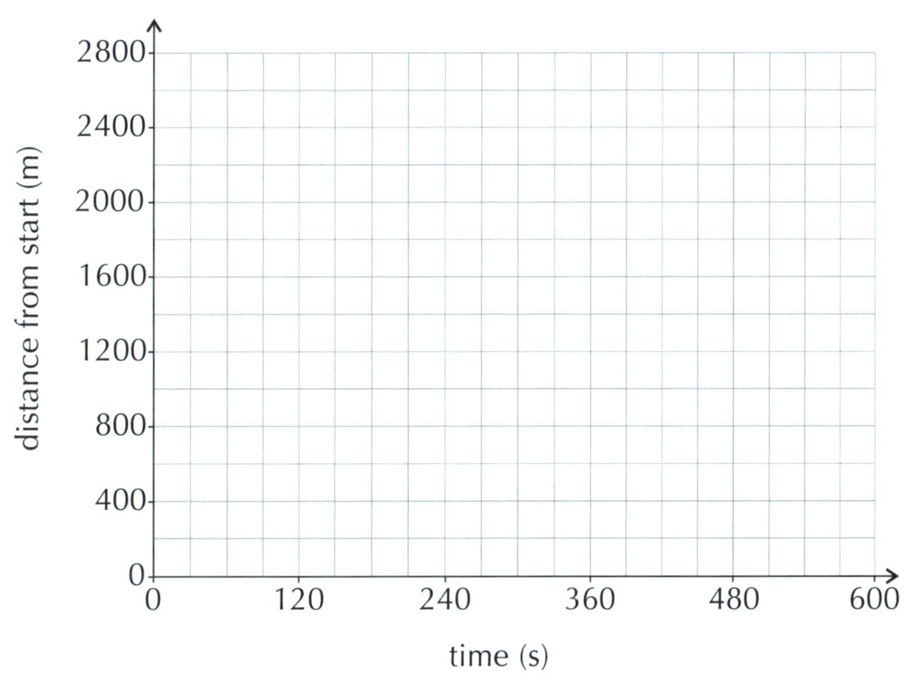

b) Radha wants a new GPS tracker that records information every second.
If Radha used this tracker, what extra information could she get from the new graph?

....

....

....

....

How did you do?

Well done, you've travelled all the way to the end of the topic. By now, you should:

- ☐ Understand how to read distance-time graphs.
- ☐ Understand how to draw your own distance-time graphs.
- ☐ Know what acceleration is.

Topic 2 — Forces

Force will get you nowhere with these questions — you'll have to rely on your brains I'm afraid.

Learning Objectives

1. Know the difference between contact forces and non-contact forces.
2. Understand when forces acting are balanced or unbalanced.
3. Be able to show the forces acting on an object using force arrows on a diagram.
4. Know how the forces acting on an object will affect (or not affect) the movement of the object.
5. Know what friction is and be able to describe how the size of frictional forces can be affected.
6. Know the effect of forces in stretching and compressing materials and understand Hooke's law.

Before you Start

1. **Are these statements true or false? Tick the correct box.**

	True	False
A force is a push or pull on an object.	☐	☐
A force only acts when two objects are touching each other.	☐	☐

2. **Complete the following sentences by drawing circles around the correct words.**

Water resistance and air resistance are forces that can **slow down / speed up** an object. This means that they are types of **drag / acceleration**. The direction of water resistance and air resistance is **the same as / opposite to** the direction of movement.

3. **Isaac needs to pull a heavy box home from the shops. Do you think the box would move more easily over dry pavement or over ice?**

☐ dry pavement ☐ ice

4. **The diagram below shows a spring.**

There are two actions listed below. Draw a line between the action and the picture that shows what you think the spring would look like after doing the action.

Pushing on both ends of the spring

Pulling on both ends of the spring

Types of Force

1. Most objects have more than one force acting on them all the time.

a) A skydiver opens his parachute. The skydiver's weight is pulling him down.
What force is acting upwards on the skydiver to slow him down?

....

b) A child is about to flick an elastic band at ~~her brother's head~~ an empty cola can. She pulls on the elastic band with her finger. What force acts on her finger in the other direction?

....

c) A ball rolling across a table slows down and stops.
What forces act in the opposite direction to the movement of the ball to slow it down?

....

2. Which of the following is a unit used to measure force? Circle the correct answer.

kilograms	newtons	metres per second	pascals	degrees of cuteness

3. Nnekay is using a magnet to pick up some paperclips from the table. The paperclips lift off the table because they're attracted to the magnet by a non-contact force.

a) What is meant by 'a non-contact force'?

....

....

Another paperclip moves across the table towards the magnet due to this force.

b) Give one contact force that acts on the paperclip as it moves across the table.

....

4. A student pulls a box along the surface of a table.

PRACTICAL

How could the student measure the size of the force they apply to the box?

....

....

....

Balanced and Unbalanced Forces

1. Which of the force diagrams below show a pair of balanced forces?
Circle all correct answers.

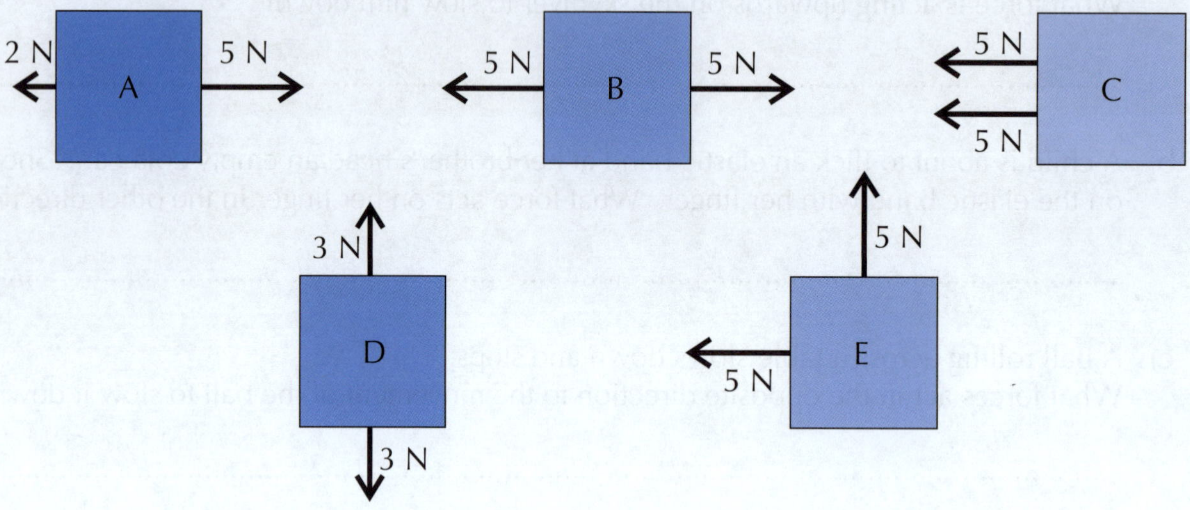

2. The diagram shows a box on a shelf.

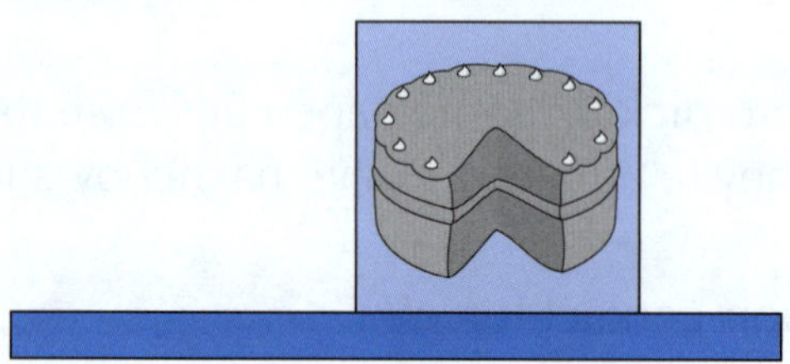

a) Draw arrows on the diagram to show the direction of the forces acting on the box.

b) Jordan pushes the box until it falls off the end of the shelf.
Jordan's friend Saskia catches the box. She says:

> When I caught the box, it stopped moving because my arms created an upward force on the box.

Do you think Saskia is right? Explain your answer.

....

....

....

Balanced and Unbalanced Forces

3. The diagram below shows two forces acting on a snail.

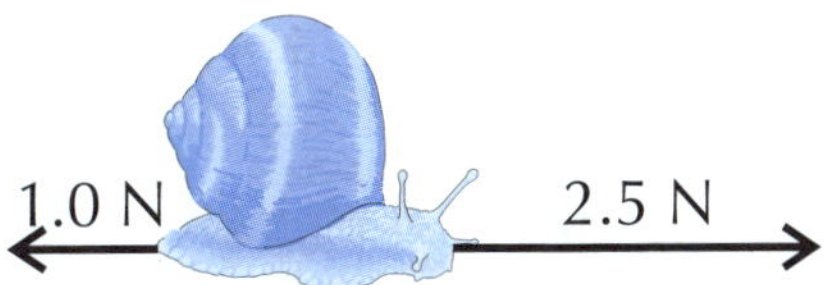

What is the size of the resultant force acting on the snail?

.... N

4. A cyclist is riding her bike along the road in a straight line at a constant speed.

a) What is the resultant force acting on the bike?

.... N

A gust of wind blows, causing a force on the bike as shown in the diagram.

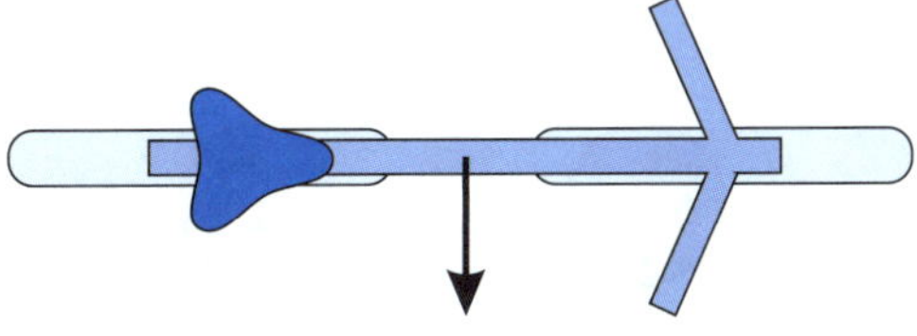

The diagram shows the bike as if you're looking down on it from above.

b) Describe how the motion of the bike changes due to the new force.

....

....

5. The force diagram shows the forces acting on a UFO.

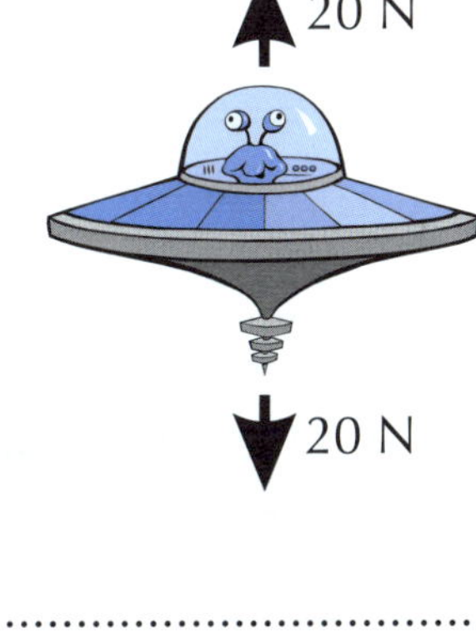

a) i) Is the UFO stationary or moving at a constant speed?

☐ stationary

☐ moving at constant speed

☐ cannot tell

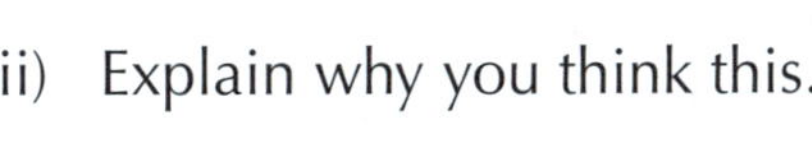

ii) Explain why you think this.

....

....

....

Balanced and Unbalanced Forces

b) The diagrams show changes in the size and direction of the forces acting on the UFO.

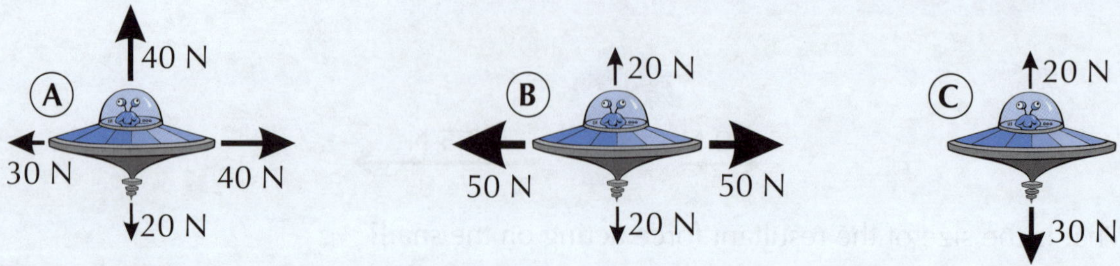

Which diagram (**A-C**) shows the biggest change in speed and direction of the UFO? Explain your answer.

....

....

6. The diagram shows the forces acting on a moving car.

Two students looked at the diagram and said the following:

Leigh: The car can't be moving because the forces acting on it are in equilibrium, so it must be still.

Petra: The car must be speeding up because there is a forward force acting on it.

a) Do you agree with Leigh, Petra, or neither of them? Explain why.

....

....

....

....

b) The forward thrust increases by 250 N. Friction and air resistance together decrease by 100 N. Calculate the resultant force acting on the car.

.... N

Friction and Resistance

1. A student was investigating the effect of friction on movement. The diagram shows the set-up for her investigation.

PRACTICAL

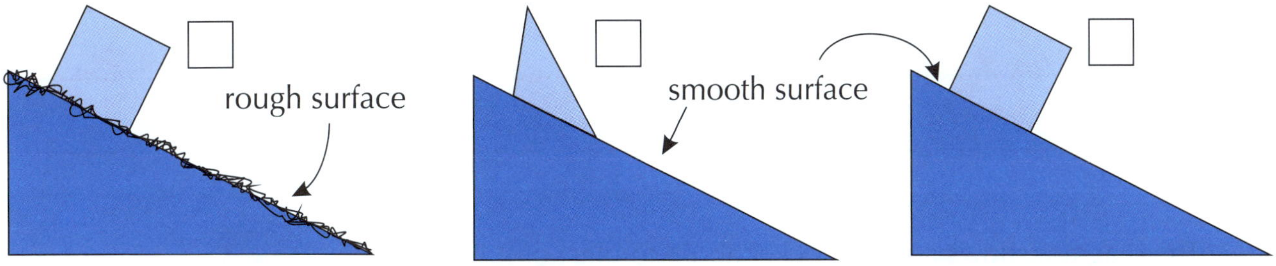

rough surface ☐ smooth surface ☐ ☐

a) All of the objects have the same mass and the same area in contact with the surface. Put the numbers 1 to 3 in the boxes next to the diagrams to show the order, from fastest to slowest, that the objects will move down the slope.

b) Is the force between the object and the slope a contact force or a non-contact force?

☐ contact force ☐ non-contact force

The student puts the last set-up in a vacuum box. The diagram below shows this set-up. Assume that friction between the box and the slope hasn't changed.

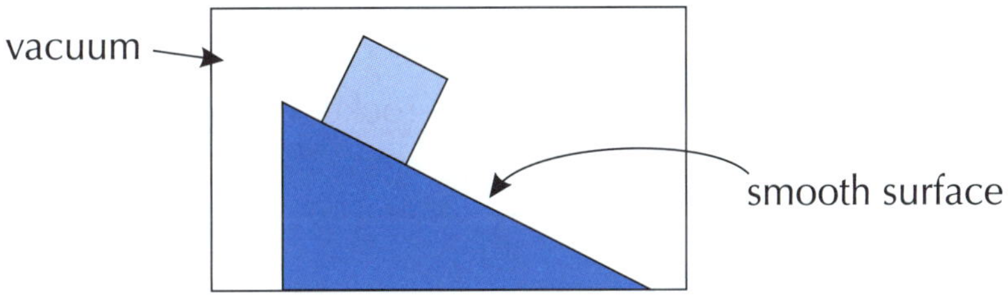

vacuum

smooth surface

c) Do you think the object will now move faster, slower, or at the same speed as it did in this set-up when it wasn't in a vacuum? Explain your answer.

....

....

....

....

2. Amita is a delivery driver for a local newsagent. She uses a van to deliver the newspapers.

a) One day, it snows. When Amita tries to drive the van on the snow, the wheels just spin and the van doesn't move forwards. Why do you think this happens?

SCIENCE IN ACTION

....

....

....

Friction and Resistance

b) Amita pushes rough pieces of board under her tyres to help her move the van. How do you think this helps the van to move?

....

....

....

3. The diagram shows a space rocket about to blast off. To be able to get into space it needs to overcome gravity and air resistance.

SCIENCE IN ACTION

a) Describe how you think the shape of the rocket helps it to overcome air resistance.

....

....

....

After some time in space, part of the rocket returns to Earth. The diagram shows how this part of the spaceship falls through the air, before and after a parachute opens.

before

after

b) Describe the changes in the size of the forces acting on this part of the rocket before and after the parachute opens.

....

....

....

....

Forces and Elasticity

1. The diagram shows a spring lying on a table and a force that is being applied to the spring. Three students looked at the diagram and suggested what would happen to the spring.

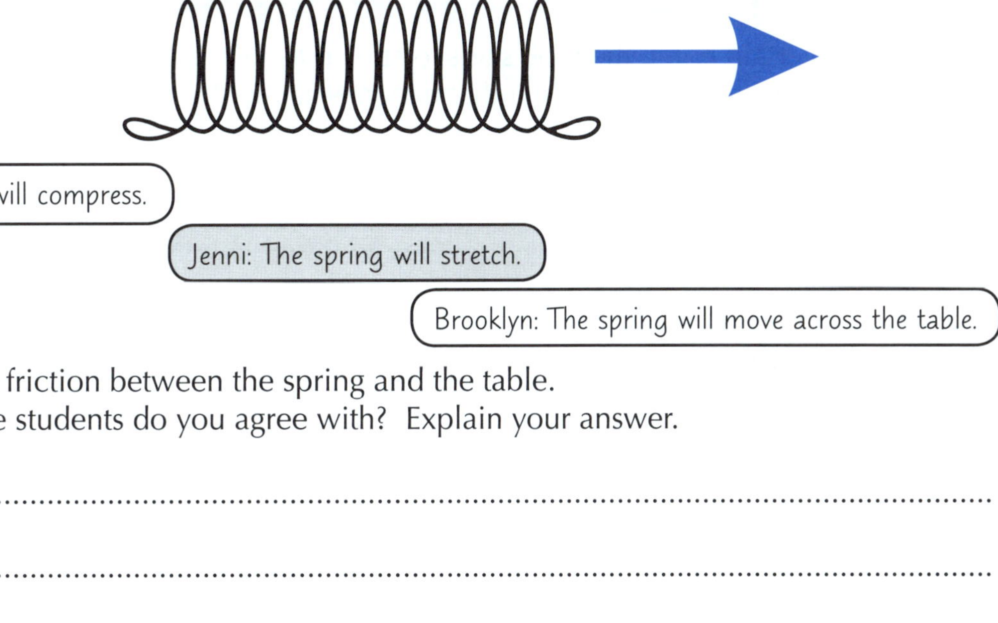

Assume there's no friction between the spring and the table.
Which of the three students do you agree with? Explain your answer.

....

....

....

2. Car suspension uses large springs that connect the wheels to the main body of the car. The diagram shows a car wheel with suspension in two situations. One approaching a speed bump and another where the car is raised off the ground so the tyre can be changed.

SCIENCE IN ACTION

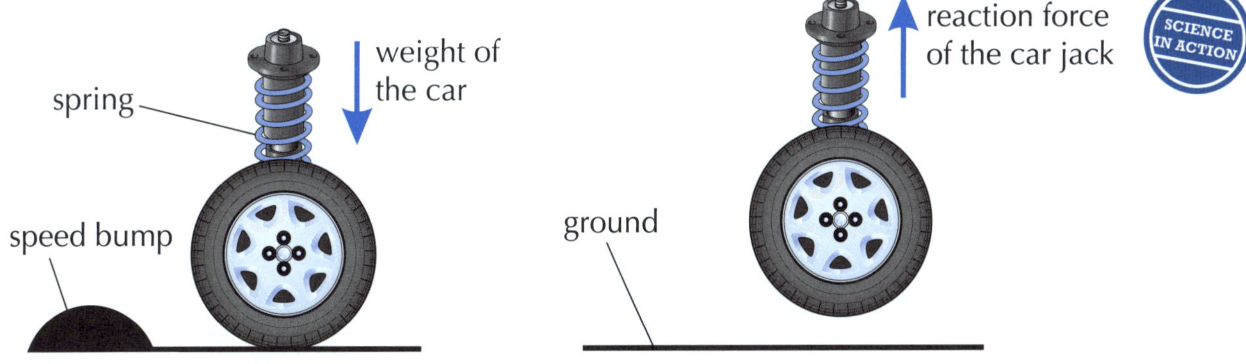

What do you think will happen to the length of the spring in each of the following situations? Explain your answer.

when the wheel moves over the speed bump: ....

....

....

when the car is raised above the ground: ....

....

....

Forces and Elasticity

3. Rochelle goes bungee jumping. An elastic rope is attached to a platform built on the edge of a cliff. The other end of this rope is then clipped onto a harness that Rochelle is wearing. Rochelle then jumps off the platform over the cliff edge.

a) At a certain point, the rope starts to stretch as Rochelle falls. Describe the energy transfer that happens as the stretching of the rope slows her down.

....

....

b) After Rochelle reaches the lowest point of the jump, she bounces back up into the air. Why does this happen?

....

....

....

4. The graph shows force against extension for a material. MATHS SKILLS

Explain how the graph shows that the material doesn't obey Hooke's law.

....

....

....

....

....

....

....

Force (N): 0, 2, 4, 6, 8
Extension (mm): 0, 5, 10, 15, 20, 25

How did you do?

I can't force you to tick off the boxes below, but I think it'd be useful. You should:

- ☐ Know the difference between contact and non-contact forces.
- ☐ Understand when forces are balanced or unbalanced.
- ☐ Be able to draw force arrows on diagrams.
- ☐ Know how forces can affect movement and shape.
- ☐ Understand the effects of friction.
- ☐ Understand Hooke's law.

Topic 3 — Gravity

Gravity is really important. Work through these questions so you understand the gravity of the situation.

Learning Objectives

1. Know that every object has a gravitational force that acts on every other object.
2. Understand the difference between weight and mass.
3. Understand how weight and mass are related to gravity.
4. Be able to calculate the weight of an object using the equation: weight = mass × gravitational field strength
5. Know that the size of gravitational force depends on mass and distance.

Before you Start

1. **Are these statements true or false? Tick the correct box.**

	True	False
Gravity won't act on you if you're standing on the ground.	☐	☐
On Earth, gravity always acts towards the centre of the Earth.	☐	☐
There are places on Earth where the force of gravity is very weak.	☐	☐
Gravity only acts if there is air.	☐	☐

2. **A student has a bank note with a mass of 1 g and a paper clip with a mass of 0.8 g. The student drops them from the same height above the ground.**

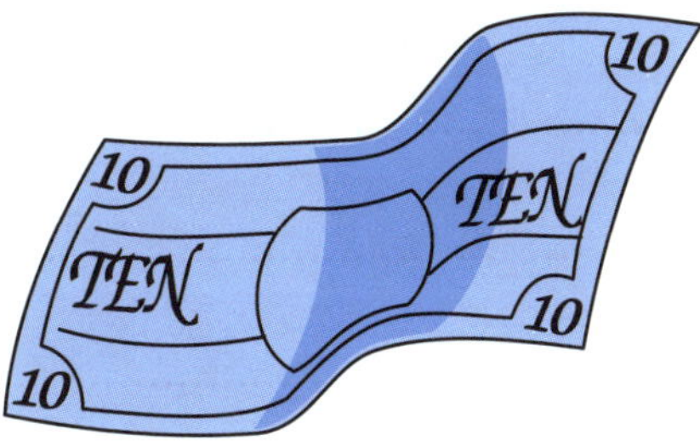

Which do you think is likely to hit the ground first?

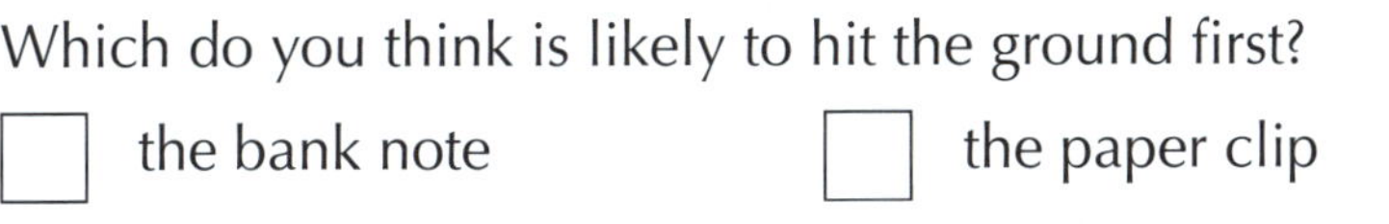

☐ the bank note ☐ the paper clip

3. **Tick the boxes next to the objects that you think exert a gravitational force.**

☐ the Earth ☐ the Sun ☐ the Moon

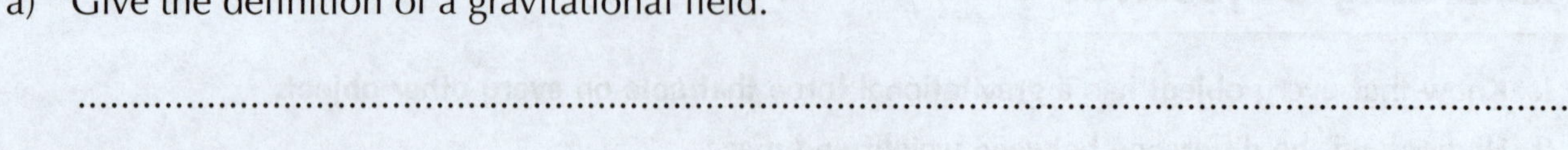

Gravity

1. All objects have a gravitational field.

a) Give the definition of a gravitational field.

....

....

b) The Earth's gravitational field causes a force that acts on a rugby ball. Which diagram shows the correct direction of this force? Tick the box by the correct diagram.

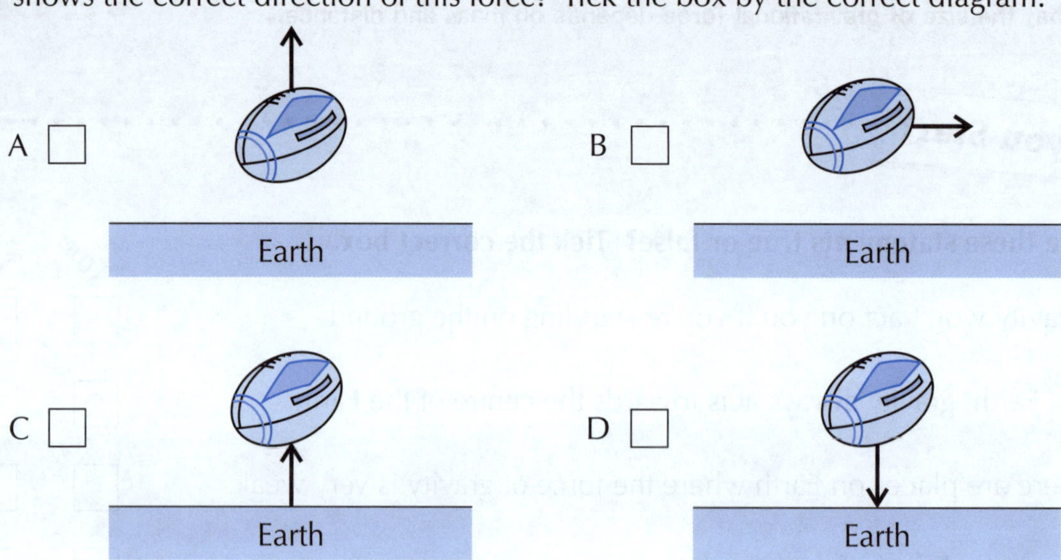

2. The weight of an object depends on the gravitational field strength.

a) What is the difference between mass and weight?

....

....

....

....

b) Which of the following is the correct definition of gravitational field strength? Tick the correct answer.

The force felt by every object in a gravitational field. ☐

The force from gravity on a 1 kg mass. ☐

The amount of stuff in an object that has a weight of 1 N. ☐

The force of gravity between the Earth and the Moon. ☐

Gravity

3. Austin is playing a game with some dice.
He drops two dice, A and B, shown on the right.

Dice A 3 g

Dice B 5 g

a) i) What is the formula that links weight, mass and gravitational field strength?

....

ii) Which dice, A or B, has the greater weight?
Explain your answer.

....

....

b) Austin says: "Dice B will hit the ground before dice A, because it has a larger mass".
Do you agree with Austin? Explain your answer.

....

....

....

c) The dice hit the floor and are at rest.
On the diagram of dice A below, draw and label all the forces acting on the dice.

floor

d) Austin has another dice, dice C, that is made of steel. Steel is a magnetic material.
He puts it away in a case which uses a magnet to hold it in place.
Describe **one** similarity and **one** difference between gravitational and magnetic forces.

Similarity = ...

....

....

Difference = ...

....

....

Gravity

4. An astronaut has a weight of 800 N on Earth.

a) i) What is the gravitational field strength on Earth?

gravitational field strength = ... N/kg

ii) Calculate the astronaut's mass. MATHS SKILLS

mass = ... kg

The astronaut goes on a mission to the Moon.
The diagram below shows part of the orbit of the Moon around Earth. The direction of the Moon's movement is always at right angles to the direction of the Earth's gravitational force.

b) How do you think gravity causes the Moon to orbit Earth? Tick the correct answer.

It has no effect on the Moon's orbit. ☐

It causes the Moon to change speed. ☐

It causes the Moon to change direction. ☐

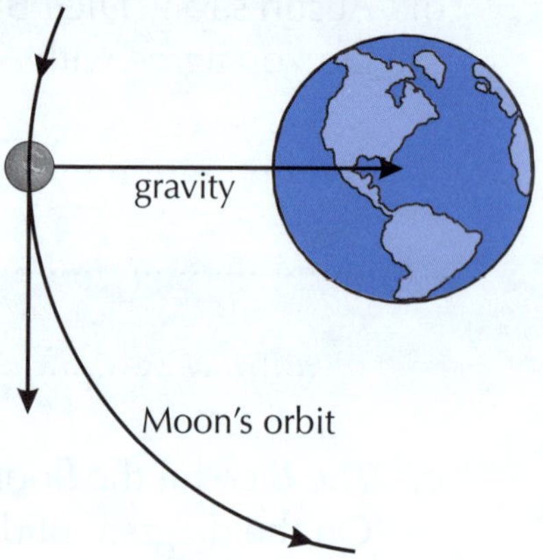

The astronaut measures her weight on the Moon.
The gravitational field strength on the Moon is 1.6 N/kg.

c) i) What is the astronaut's mass on the Moon?

mass = ... kg

ii) What is the astronaut's weight on the Moon? MATHS SKILLS

weight = ... N

The astronaut travels back to Earth on a rocket. The rocket travels in a straight line from the surface of the Moon to the surface of the Earth, as shown in the diagram.
In order for the rocket to take off from the Moon, it has to apply a large force. Once the rocket has moved some distance away from the Moon, it no longer needs to apply this force.

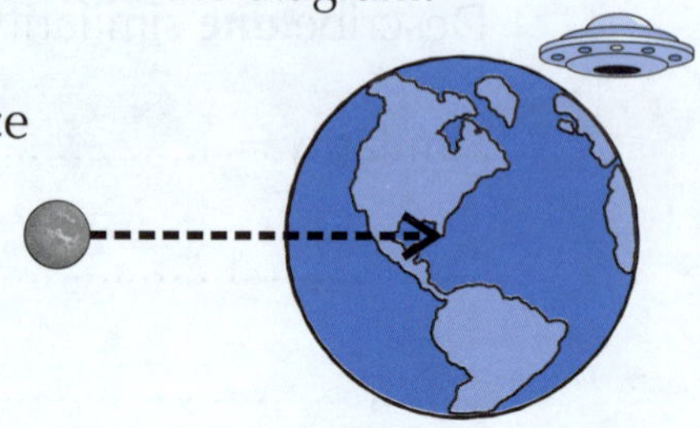

d) Explain, in terms of gravity, why the rocket does not need to constantly apply the force.

....

....

....

Gravity

5. Veronica is a mountain climber. On one of her expeditions, she decides to do an experiment to see how the weight of an object changes based on her height up the mountain.

PRACTICAL

She measures the weight of a 1.0 kg ball each time she gets 500 m higher above the base of the mountain. Her results are shown on the graph below.

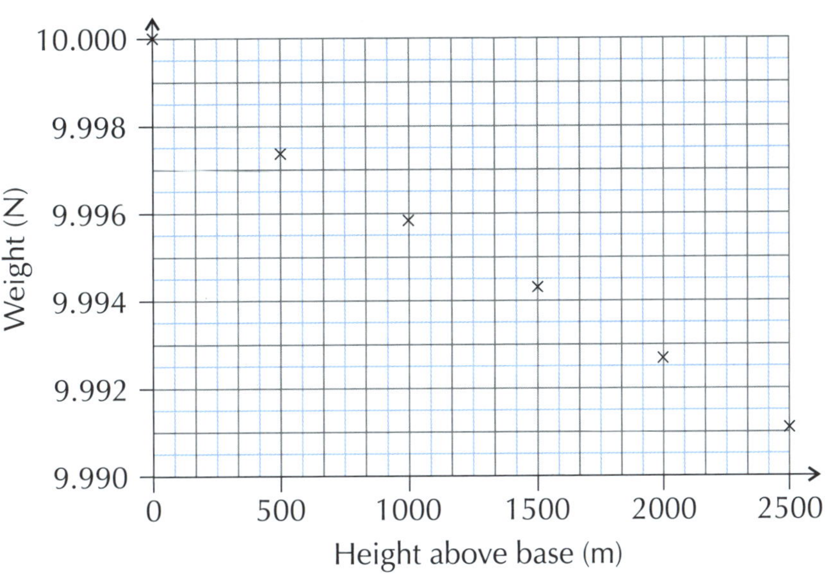

MATHS SKILLS

a) Describe the trend shown by the graph.

....

b) Explain the trend of the graph in terms of gravity.

....

....

....

c) Veronica repeats the experiment with a ball with twice the mass. How would the graph of results for this experiment be different to the graph shown above? Explain why.

....

....

....

How did you do?

Whew, gravity can't seem to keep you down. After answering all those questions you should:

- ☐ Understand there's a gravitational force between all objects with mass.
- ☐ Understand how weight, mass and gravity are related.
- ☐ Understand the difference between weight and mass.
- ☐ Be able to calculate an object's weight from its mass and the gravitational field strength.

Topic 4 — Circuits

You might remember circuits from Year 7 — well, as circuits do, they've come around again.

Learning Objectives

1. Be able to calculate resistance from the potential difference (voltage) and current.
2. Be able to draw a circuit diagram to show how the voltage in a circuit can be measured.
3. Know that in a series circuit current is the same everywhere.
4. Know that in a series circuit voltage is shared between components.
5. Know that in parallel circuits the current divides at loops before combining again.
6. Know that each loop in a parallel circuit has the same voltage.

Before you Start

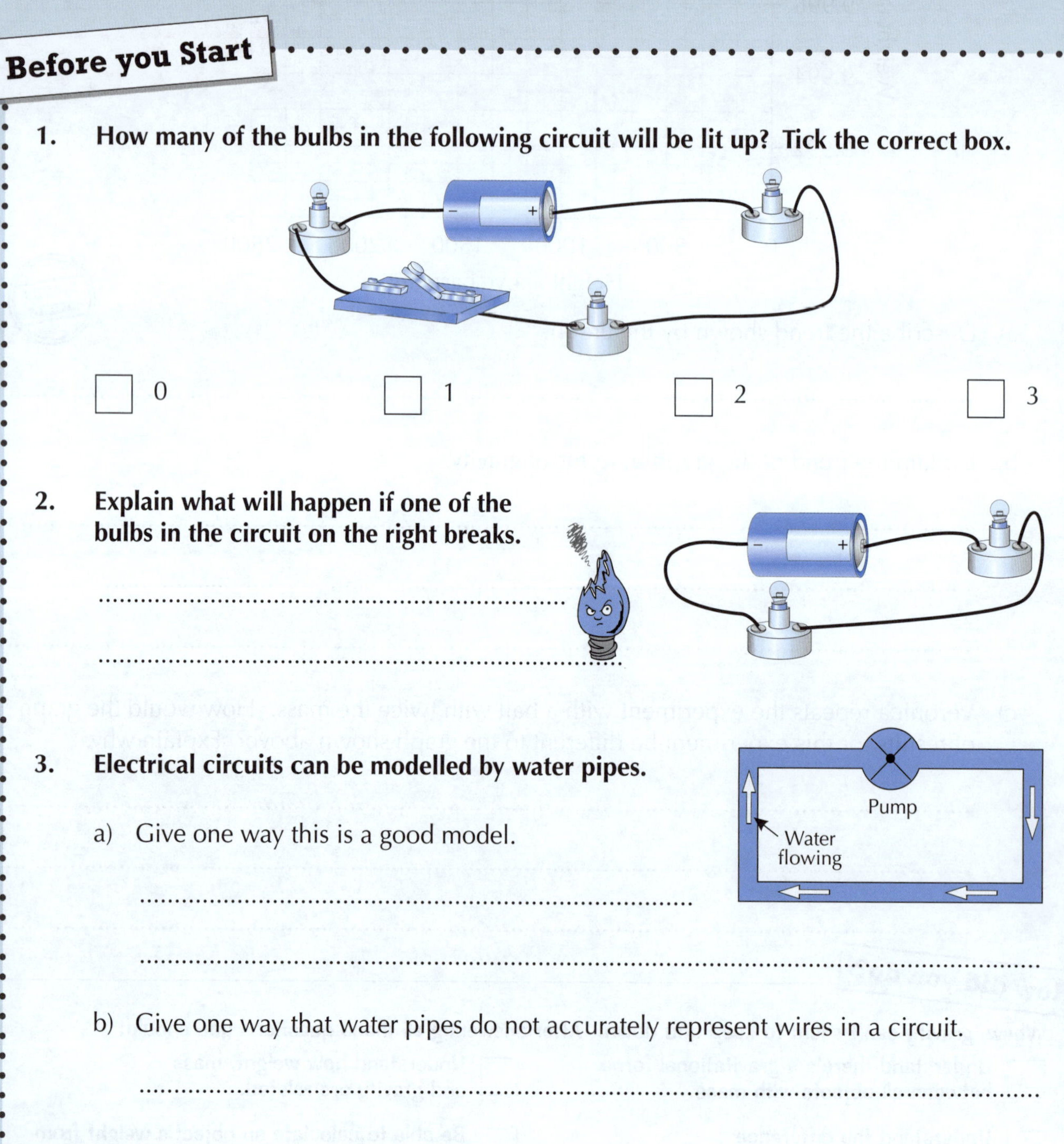

1. **How many of the bulbs in the following circuit will be lit up? Tick the correct box.**

☐ 0 ☐ 1 ☐ 2 ☐ 3

2. **Explain what will happen if one of the bulbs in the circuit on the right breaks.**

....

....

3. **Electrical circuits can be modelled by water pipes.**

a) Give one way this is a good model.

....

....

b) Give one way that water pipes do not accurately represent wires in a circuit.

....

....

Resistance

1. Which of the following is correct?

☐ Resistance = Potential Difference ÷ Current

☐ Resistance = Current ÷ Potential Difference

☐ Resistance = Potential Difference × Current

2. Romesh uses the circuit shown below to test the resistances of three materials. Each piece of material that he tests is exactly the same size. His results are shown in the table.

Material	Resistance (Ω)
1	150
2	5.5
3	14

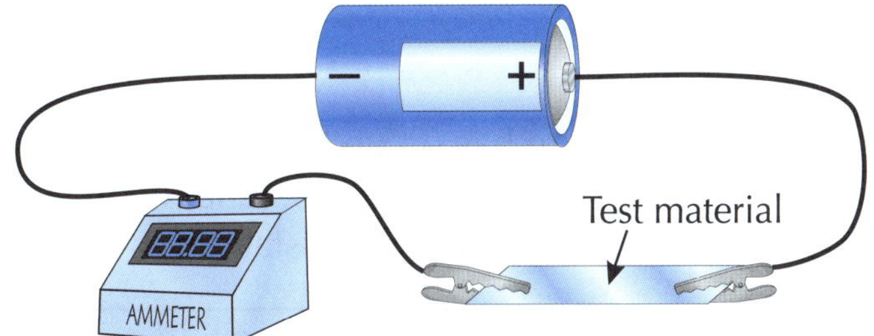

a) Which material had the highest current flowing through it?

....

b) Which material is the worst electrical conductor?

....

c) Romesh used a battery with a potential difference rating of 6 V.
What is the maximum possible potential difference across the test material?

....

3. Claire sets up a test circuit. A circuit diagram of her circuit is shown below.

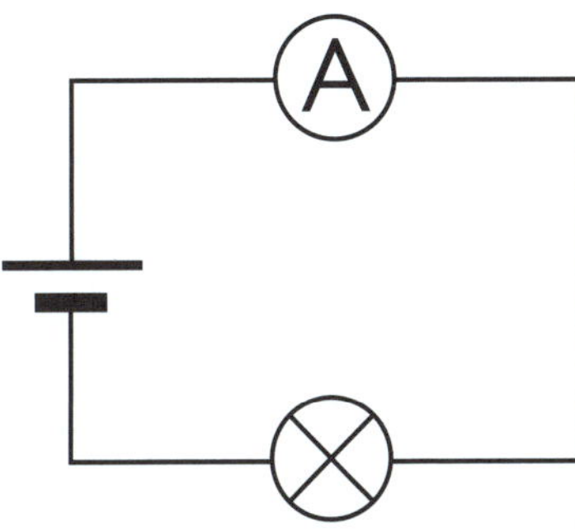

Resistance

a) Claire is using an ammeter to measure the current but she also wants to measure the potential difference across the bulb. Draw a new circuit diagram to show how she could do that.

b) Once Claire has set up her new circuit she uses different cells to change the potential difference across the bulb. She records the current each time. Her results are shown below. Calculate the resistances to complete the table. One has been done for you.

Potential difference (V)	Current (A)	Resistance (Ω)
1	0.25	....
2	0.40	....
3	0.50	....
4	0.58	6.9

c) Why was it important for Claire to check the potential difference rating of the bulb before conducting her experiment?

....

....

....

d) Claire's teacher also told Claire to make sure the current didn't get too high. Explain why a large current in the circuit is a potential safety risk.

....

....

....

Series Circuits

1. The statements below are about the circuit diagram shown.
Write **true** or **false** next to each sentence to show whether it is correct or not.

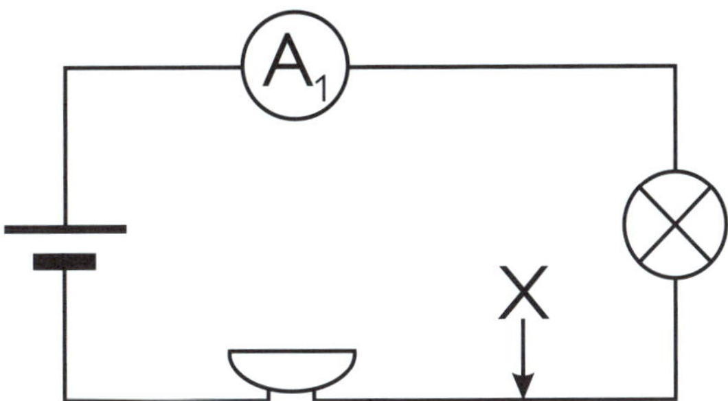

The circuit is a series circuit. ....

If a bulb was added at position X the circuit would be a parallel circuit. ....

If the ammeter was moved to position X,
the reading on A_1 would be different. ....

The total of the potential differences across the bulb and the buzzer
will be the same as the potential difference rating of the cell. ....

2. Paula and Kai are discussing the circuit shown below:

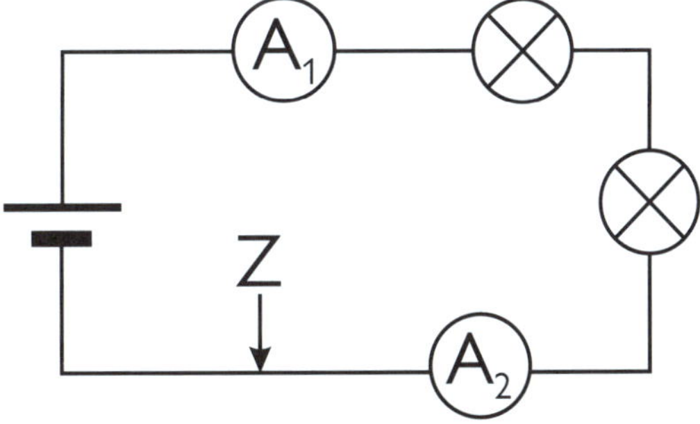

Paula: I think the current is shared between each component, so I think the current through each bulb will add up to the reading on A_1.

Kai: I think that the current gets used up by each of the bulbs, so the current at A_1 must be lower than at A_2.

a) Explain how far you agree with:

i) Paula ....

....

....

Series Circuits

ii) Kai ....

....

....

b) Another bulb is added to the circuit at position Z.

i) What will happen to the readings on A_1 and A_2? Explain your answer.

....

....

....

ii) Before the bulb is added, Kai says:

I expect the bulbs to be dimmer when the third bulb is added.

Explain how far you agree with Kai.

....

....

....

....

3. Taylor measured the potential difference across two resistors in the circuit below.

a) V_1 reads 7 V. What is the potential difference across resistor 2?

....

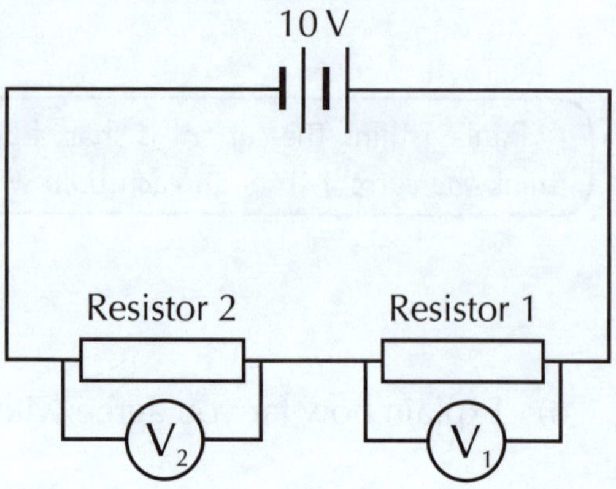

b) Which resistor has the greater resistance? Explain your answer.

....

....

....

....

Parallel Circuits

1. When all the switches in the circuit shown are closed, all the motors run.

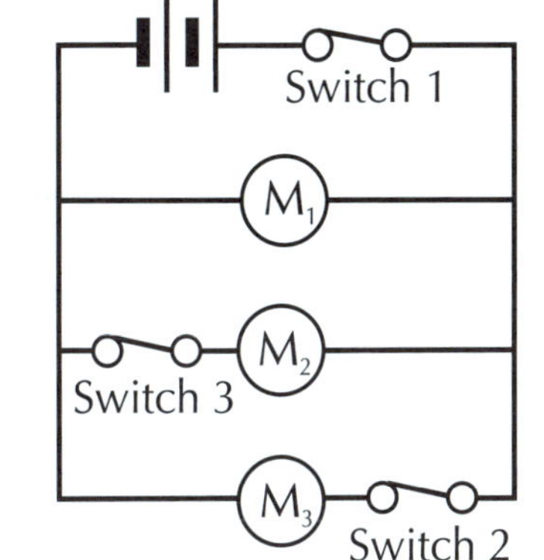

a) Which of the motors will run if only switch 1 is open?

....

b) Which of the motors will run if only switch 2 is open?

....

c) Which of the motors will run if only switch 3 is open?

....

d) What feature of the circuit shows that it is a parallel circuit?

....

2. Antonio is making a doll's house. Antonio builds a circuit for the lights in each room.

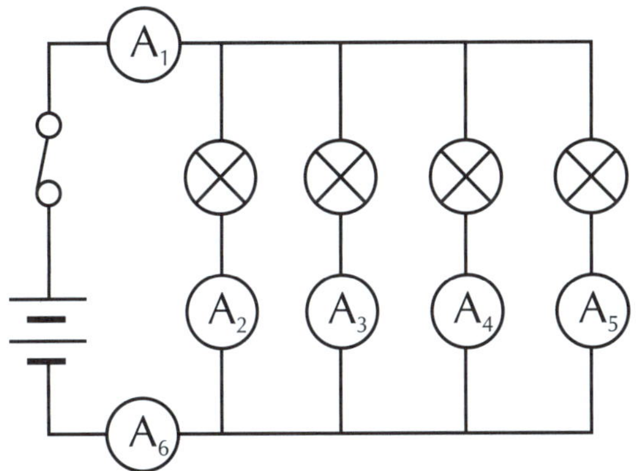

Ammeter	Current (A)
A_1	12
A_2	5
A_3	1
A_4	2
A_5	....
A_6	....

a) The readings from A_1 to A_4 are shown in the table. Enter the values for A_5 and A_6 to complete the table.

b) Antonio wants to be able to turn the bulbs in each room on and off individually. Where should he put switches so that he can do this?

....

....

c) Give one other reason that using a parallel circuit is better than connecting the bulbs in one loop.

....

....

Parallel Circuits

3. Erin's teacher shows her two circuits. Both circuits use identical bulbs.

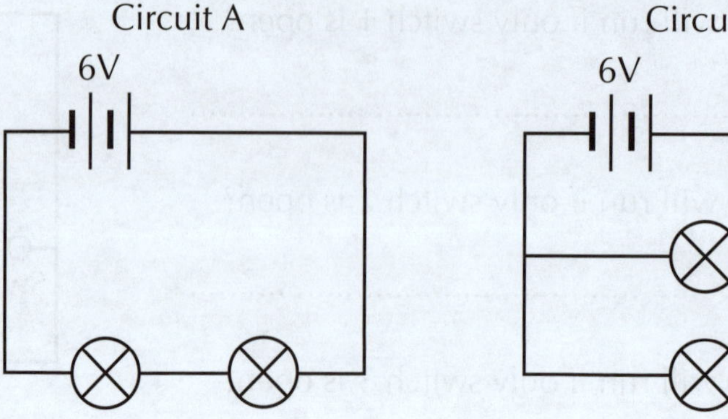

a) Which circuit will have the larger potential difference across each bulb? Explain your answer.

....

....

....

....

b) Erin's teacher adds an extra loop to circuit B and adds a bulb on that loop. Erin says she doesn't expect the brightness of the bulbs to change. Explain how far you agree.

....

....

....

c) Erin's teacher then changes the battery in circuit B to one with a potential difference rating of 12 V, which is still lower than the potential difference rating of the bulbs. What would you expect to happen to the brightness of the bulbs? Explain your answer.

....

....

....

How did you do?

Hopefully everything's a little brighter now and you're not still in the dark about circuits. Make sure you:

- ☐ **Know how to calculate resistance.**
- ☐ **Can draw a circuit diagram.**
- ☐ **Understand voltage and current in series and parallel circuits.**
- ☐ **Understand how changing components in circuits changes the current.**

Topic 5 — Light and Vision

Don't look so serious — lighten up a bit. Get ready to learn about light and vision.

Learning Objectives

1. Understand how light is refracted when it enters a medium of a different density.
2. Draw ray diagrams to show refraction.
3. Know how different parts of the eye work together to create an image to send to the brain.
4. Understand how concave and convex lenses refract light, and their role in vision.
5. Understand how the colour of light depends on its frequency, how white light is formed, and why objects appear certain colours.

Before you Start

1. Below are particle models for glass and water.

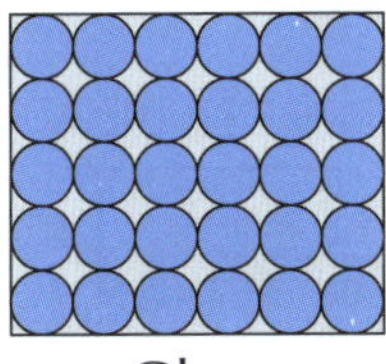
Glass

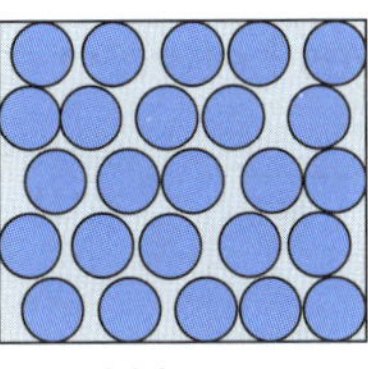
Water

Which would you expect to be less dense?

....

2. Circle the correct diagram showing a ray of light being reflected by a mirror.

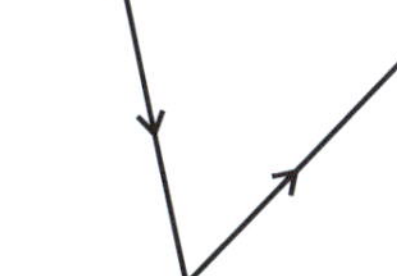

3. Use the words in the box below to fill in the gaps in the sentences below.

transparent	reflected	translucent	absorbed	reflected	transmitted

Light can be absorbed, reflected or transmitted at a boundary between materials.

When light is .... , energy is transferred to the material.

When light is .... , it passes through the material — the material has to be .... or .... When light is .... it bounces back. An object can be seen due to the light that is .... by it.

Refraction

1. Refraction is when light changes direction as it moves from one medium to another.

a) What is meant by 'medium' in the sentence above?

....

b) Which is more dense, air or glass?

....

c) Fill in the gaps to complete the sentences below.

When light moves from air to glass it bends .... the normal.

d) Complete the diagrams below to show what happens to light when it moves between media.

i)

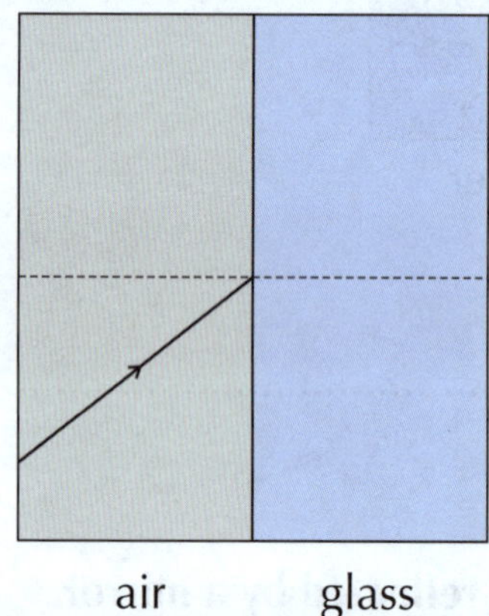

ii)

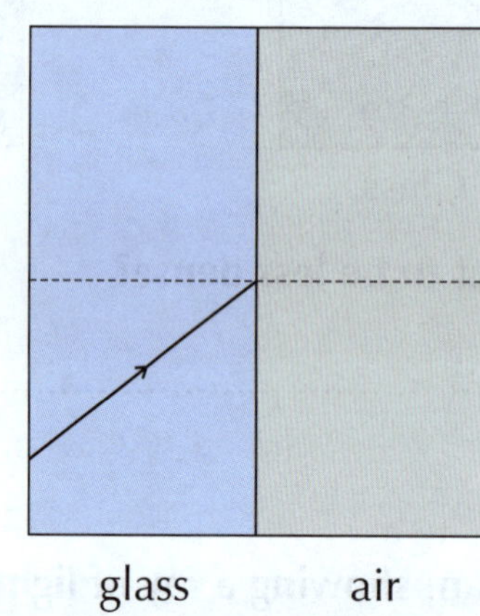

iii)

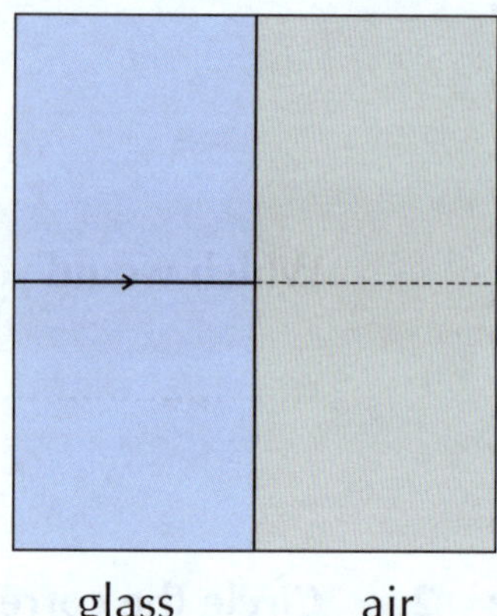

e) Complete the diagram below to show what happens when light travels from air to water, and then into glass.

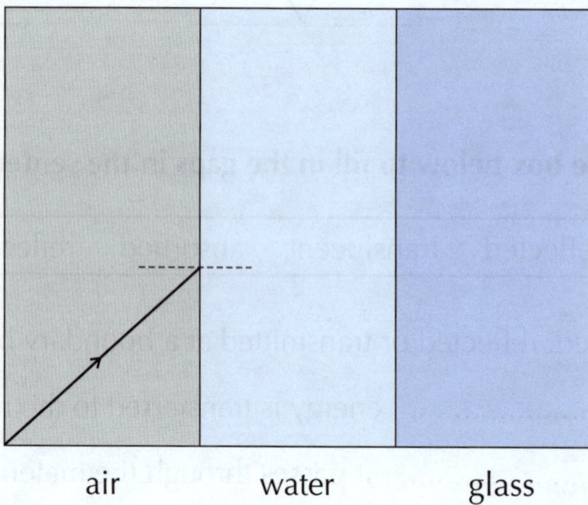

Refraction

2. An eagle can catch a fish from the water using its talons.

SCIENCE IN ACTION

The diagram shows how the fish appears to be shallower than it actually is when viewed by the eagle, due to refraction. The eagle has to account for this to catch the fish.

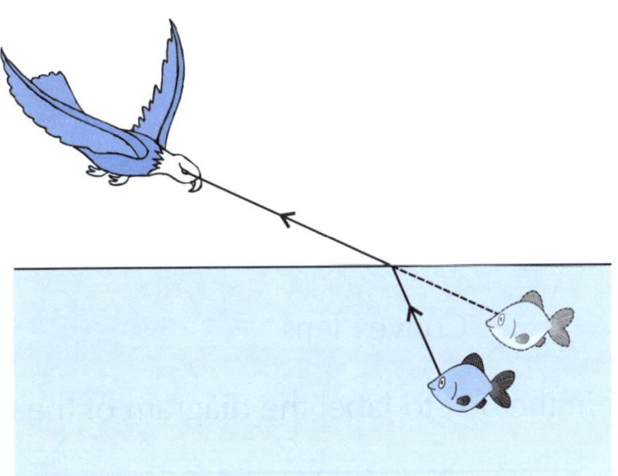

a) i) Draw the normal line on the diagram above.

ii) Label the angle of incidence on the diagram.

b) How can you tell that water is denser than air from this diagram?

....

c) If the fish swam closer to the surface, would the image of the fish that the eagle sees be closer or further away from the fish?

....

d) Complete the diagram below to show that the eagle appears much higher in the sky to the fish than it actually is.

Don't worry if you can't draw the eagle very well — it's the rays that are the important bit.

Vision

1. Lenses can be concave or convex.

a) Complete the ray diagram below to show how a **convex** lens focuses light rays.

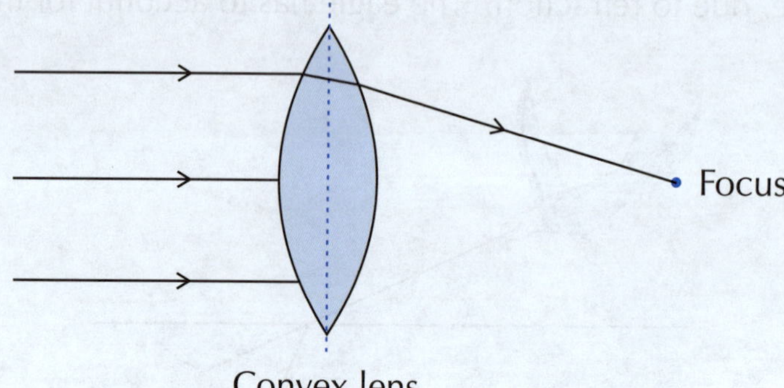

Convex lens

b) Use the words given in the box to label the diagram of the eye below.

lens	retina	cornea

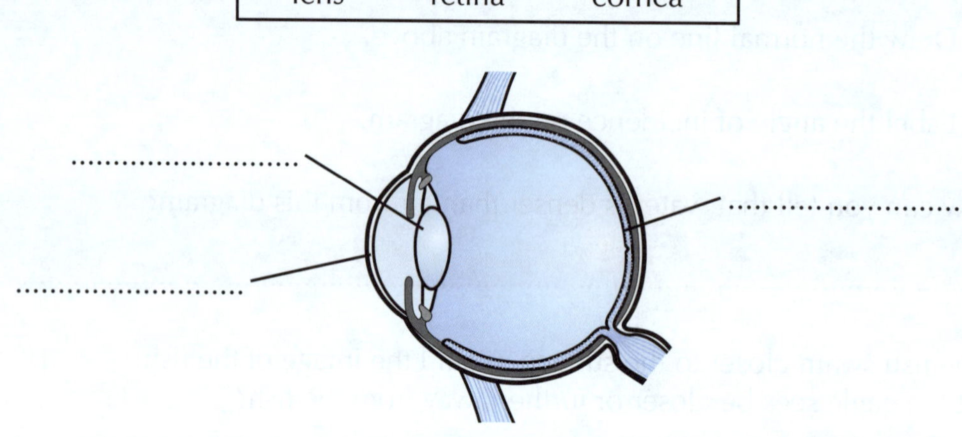

c) What does a **concave** lens do to light that passes through it?

....

d) Draw a diagram showing a concave lens.

Vision

2. Volkan likes lizards.

Below is a diagram showing a lizard, a light bulb and Volkan's eye.

a) Is the lens in a human eye concave or convex?

....

b) Complete the ray diagram showing how an image is formed on Volkan's retina.

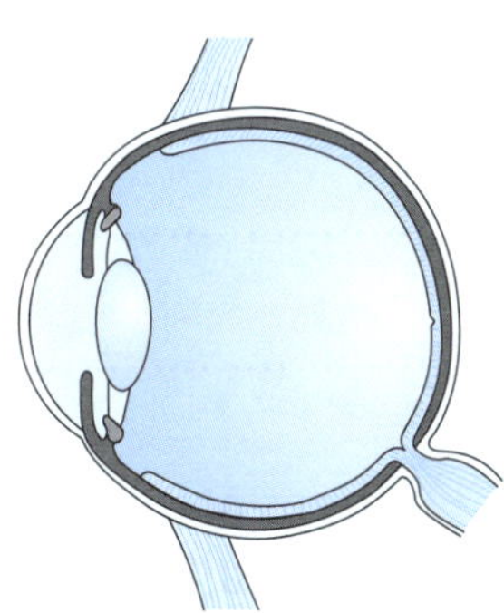

c) Describe what happens after light hits the retina of Volkan's eye.

....

3. Light transfers energy from a light source to an absorber.

a) What is an example of a light source?

....

b) Circle the correct words to complete the passage below.

In the eye, the **retina / cornea** is the absorber.

This part of the eye is **photosensitive** / **reflective**, meaning it reacts to light hitting it.

This causes chemical and **electrical** / **gravitational** changes.

Another example of an absorber is a **camera lens / camera sensor**.

Vision

4. The eye has many different parts that work together to provide sight.

For an image to be seen sharply, light must be focused exactly on the retina by the lens and cornea. The eye can change where light is focused by changing the shape of its lens using muscles. Some people have vision problems that mean their eyes cannot focus light onto the retina naturally.
Near-sightedness is where light is focused before it reaches the retina, so the image on the retina is out of focus and blurry.

a) Which option do you think could cause near-sightedness? Tick one box.

☐ The eye lens doesn't refract light.

☐ The eye lens is concave.

☐ The eyeball is too long.

☐ The retina cells aren't reactive to light.

b) Suggest why changing the shape of the lens is useful.

....

....

c) Glasses are used to correct vision problems such as near-sightedness. Glasses allow lenses to be placed in front of the eye.

The diagrams below show how an eye with perfect vision focuses light and how a near-sighted eye focuses light.

perfect vision

near-sighted

What kind of lens do you think should be used to correct near-sighted vision? Explain why.

....

....

....

Colour

1. The diagram below shows white light passing through a glass prism.

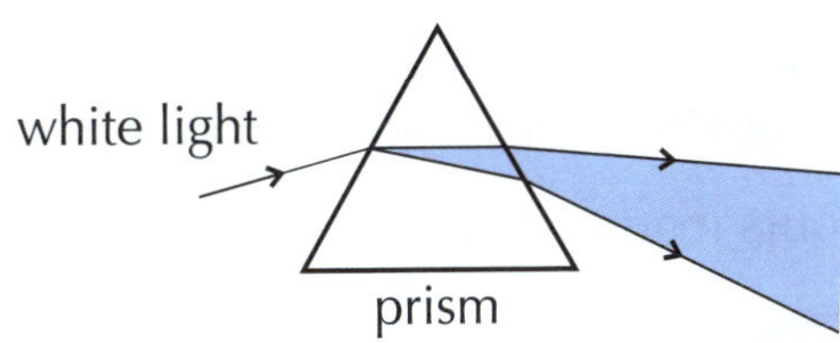

a) Describe what the light coming out of the prism would look like.

....

b) Complete the sentences below.

Different colours of light have different ....

(the number of waves that pass through a point per second).

.... light is made up of all the other colours mixed together.

c) Explain why the effect described in part a) happens.

....

2. An experiment is set up to investigate how different coloured lights affect the colour an object appears. In a dark room, a single white light is set up to shine on an object. A red or green filter is used to change the colour of the light shining on the object.

a) Fill in the table below to show what colour the objects should appear during the experiment and what colours of light the objects absorb.

Event	Colour that object appears	Colour(s) absorbed
White light hits a white object		
Green light hits a white object		None
White light hits a blue object		
Red light hits a blue object	Black	

b) The student doing the experiment gets different results. The blue object appears blue under the red light. What do you think was wrong with her method?

....

....

Colour

3. A theatre company uses blue, red and green lights to light their stage.

Red, green and blue are known as the primary colours of light because you can make all colours by mixing them together differently.

The diagram shows the colours made when red, green and blue light mix.

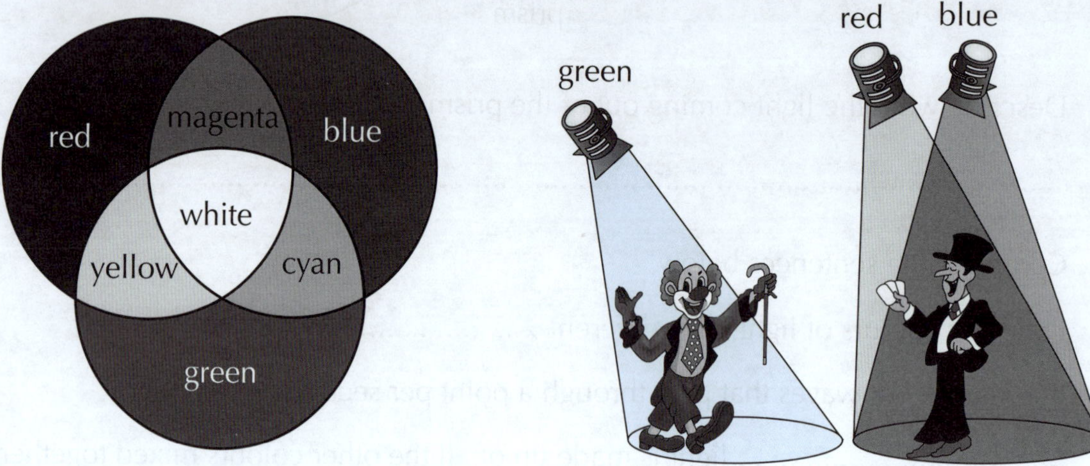

a) A sound technician says, "a red filter changes the frequency of white light to make it red". Explain why he's wrong.

....

....

b) Use the colour diagram to work out what colour light will shine on the magician.

....

c) One of the performers is wearing blue boots with red laces, but they both appear black. Which performer is it?

....

d) How could the theatre use the three lights to light the stage with white light?

....

How did you do?

That's light and vision all wrapped up. Now that this section is finished you should:

- ☐ Know how light is refracted and how to draw ray diagrams to show this.
- ☐ Understand how concave and convex lenses refract light.
- ☐ Understand how the eye works.
- ☐ Know that the colour of light depends on its frequency.
- ☐ Know what white light is.
- ☐ Understand why objects appear certain colours in certain lights.

Topic 6 — Wave Effects

It's time for some waves. How they work, what they can do and what we use them for.

Learning Objectives

1. Know that energy is transferred by waves and that the amount depends on the amplitude or frequency.
2. Understand that some high frequency waves, such as ultraviolet, can cause damage to living cells.
3. Know how a wave travels through the particles of a substance.
4. Know what is meant by a pressure wave and be able to give examples and understand their uses, including ultrasound for cleaning and physiotherapy.
5. Understand how microphones and loudspeakers convert between sound waves and electrical signals.

Before you Start

1. **Draw lines to connect the words about waves with their definitions.**

Amplitude	The displacement from the rest position to the crest of the wave.
Frequency	The distance between two peaks of a wave.
Wavelength	The number of waves per second.

2. **Which sentence best describes a sound wave? Tick the correct answer.**

☐ A longitudinal wave with vibrations in the direction of wave travel.

☐ A transverse wave with vibrations at right angles to the direction of wave travel.

3. **Fill in the table below, with the words given, to show how sound travels through different media.**

Air Wood A vacuum Water

Sound cannot travel through...	Sound can travel though...		

4. **Below are particle diagrams for three substances. Which substance do you think sound will travel fastest through? Circle the correct option.**

Waves and Energy

1. Sound waves transfer energy to make our eardrums vibrate.

a) State whether each of the following statements is true or false.

i) Waves transfer energy in the same direction the wave is travelling. ....

ii) A wave with a greater amplitude will transfer more energy. ....

iii) A wave with a greater frequency will transfer less energy. ....

b) i) The eardrum can be damaged by sound waves with a lot of energy.
What type of sound do you think is most likely to damage the eardrum?

☐ high pitched and loud ☐ high pitched and quiet

☐ low pitched and loud ☐ low pitched and quiet

ii) Explain why this type of sound is most likely to be damaging to eardrums.

....

....

2. Read the passage below and answer the questions that follow.

> Ultraviolet is a wave similar to visible light that can cause damage to skin cells. Visible light can cause burns if it's really intense (for example in lasers or if it's focused by a lens), but it can't damage cells in the same way as ultraviolet light. X-rays are another kind of wave similar to ultraviolet. X-rays have a higher frequency than ultraviolet light.

a) What are two differences between visible light and ultraviolet that are not given in the passage?

....

....

b) Why do you think visible light doesn't cause damage to skin cells like ultraviolet does?

....

....

c) What effect do you think X-rays will have on living cells?

....

....

Waves and Energy

3. Surface water waves are caused by the wind blowing over the surface of water. The energy from the waves can be used to generate electricity using wave energy converters like the one shown.

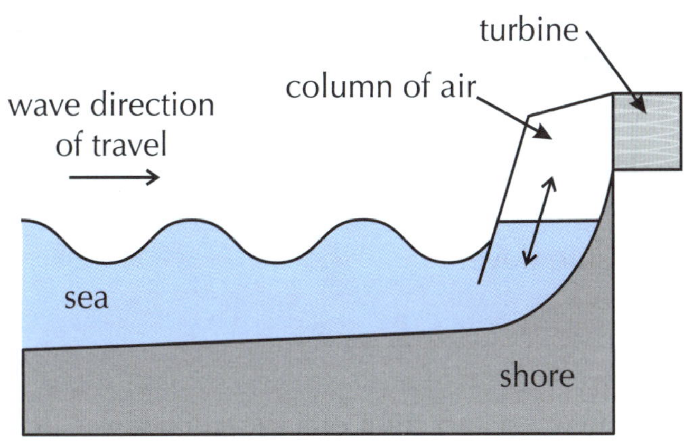

a) Circle the correct words to complete the sentences to explain how the water wave transfers energy to the turbine.

The particles of the wave move **back and forth / up and down** . When the wave reaches the wave energy converter it transfers **energy / water particles** to the air particles. A **water wave / pressure wave** is formed in the air.

This wave transfers **water particles / energy** to the turbine.

b) What effect do you think increasing the height of the waves will have on their power? Explain your answer.

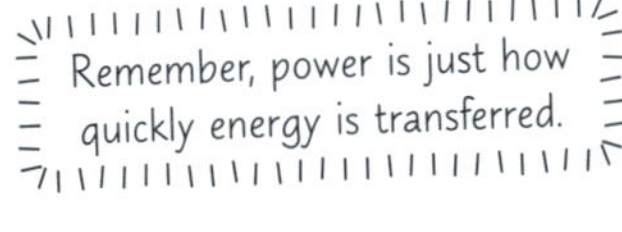

....

....

....

c) A company is choosing a location to set up wave energy converters. They know that increased wind speed causes bigger waves. Which location do you think will produce the most electrical power over time? Why?

Location	Average Wind Speed (m/s)
A	8
B	6
C	11

....

....

....

Pressure Waves

1. Sound waves are an example of a pressure wave.
The diagram shows a sound wave travelling through the particles in air.

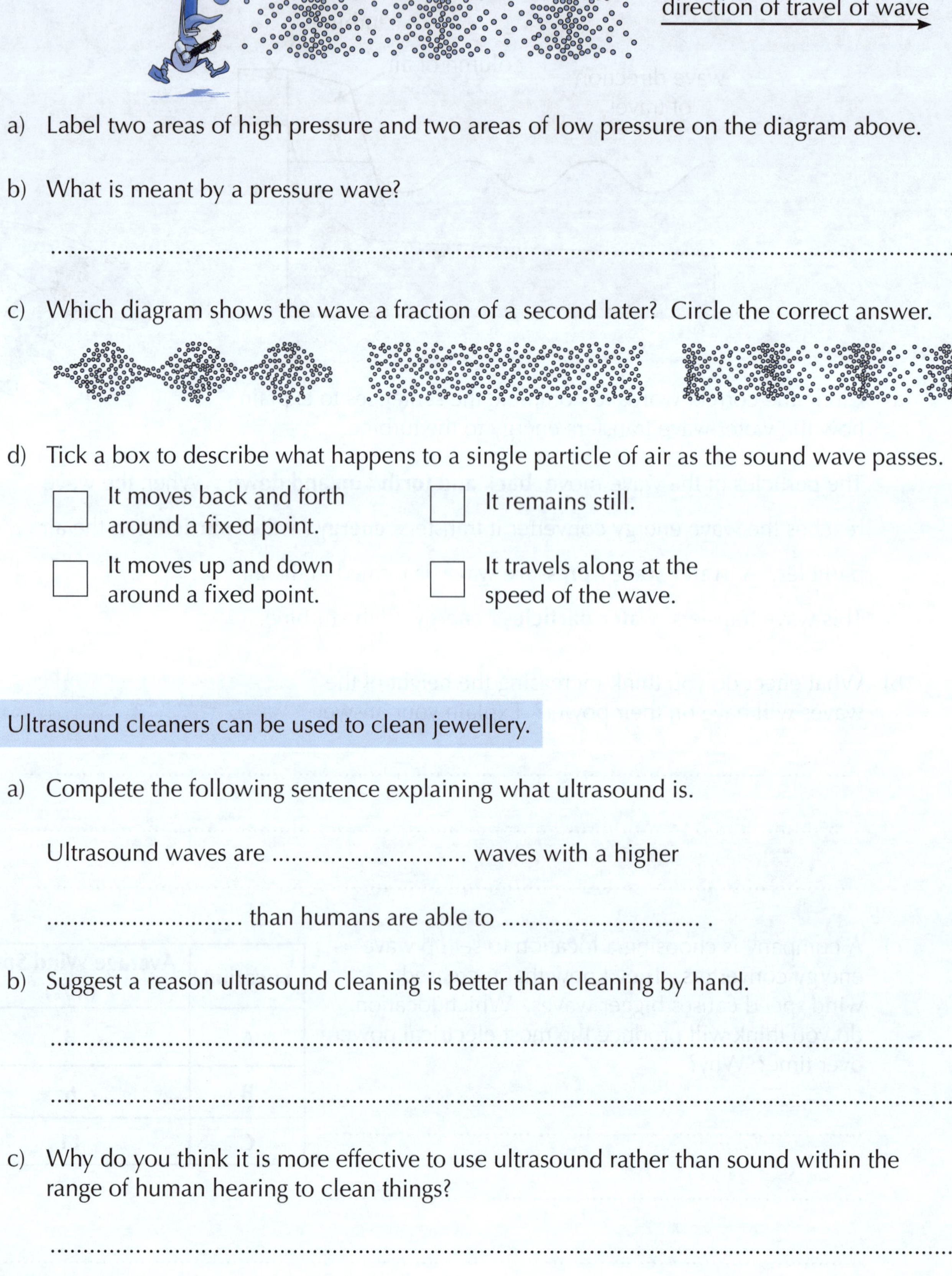

a) Label two areas of high pressure and two areas of low pressure on the diagram above.

b) What is meant by a pressure wave?

....

c) Which diagram shows the wave a fraction of a second later? Circle the correct answer.

d) Tick a box to describe what happens to a single particle of air as the sound wave passes.

- [ ] It moves back and forth around a fixed point.
- [ ] It remains still.
- [ ] It moves up and down around a fixed point.
- [ ] It travels along at the speed of the wave.

2. Ultrasound cleaners can be used to clean jewellery.

a) Complete the following sentence explaining what ultrasound is.

Ultrasound waves are .... waves with a higher

.... than humans are able to ....

b) Suggest a reason ultrasound cleaning is better than cleaning by hand.

....

....

c) Why do you think it is more effective to use ultrasound rather than sound within the range of human hearing to clean things?

....

....

Pressure Waves

3. A student says, "microphones are the opposite of loudspeakers". Explain what this means.

....

....

4. Physiotherapists can treat muscle pain with massage techniques in which they use their hands to apply pressure to parts of the body. Ultrasound can also be used to massage muscles.

SCIENCE IN ACTION

a) Fill in the gaps to complete the sentences below.

An ultrasound wave travels through a substance via .... in the substance vibrating .... and .... and hitting other particles, causing them to start .... This causes areas of .... and .... to move through the material, which is how the wave travels.

b) Ultrasound can massage deep tissue inside the body that regular massage can't reach. Explain how ultrasound transfers energy to deep tissue when ultrasound waves are created at the skin's surface.

....

....

....

c) Ultrasound travels at different speeds through different media. Knowing that ultrasound waves are pressure waves, explain whether ultrasound will travel quicker through muscle (made up of solids and liquids) or air cavities in the body.

....

....

....

How did you do?

All waves transfer energy, which can either be really useful or really dangerous. By now, you should:

- ☐ Know that the energy transferred by a wave depends on its amplitude and frequency.
- ☐ Understand how waves can damage cells.
- ☐ Know how a wave travels through a substance's particles.
- ☐ Know what a pressure wave is and understand examples and uses.
- ☐ Understand how microphones and loudspeakers work.

Topic 7 — Separating Mixtures

Some mixtures are a piece of cake to separate — cake mixture, not so much...

Learning Objectives

1. Know that the choice of separation method depends on the substances being separated.
2. Understand that filtration can be used to separate insoluble solids from liquids.
3. Understand that evaporation can be used to separate dissolved solids from liquids.
4. Understand that chromatography can be used to separate and identify substances.
5. Know that distillation works because liquids have different boiling points.

Before you Start

1. **Sort these substances into the table below.**

nitrogen gas　　fruit juice　　milk

seawater　　air　　diamond

Pure Substance	Mixture

2. **Tick all the true sentences about pure substances and mixtures.**

☐ A pure substance has a fixed melting point.

☐ Melting and boiling points can be used to help identify pure substances.

☐ Mixtures can only be separated if they are liquids or gases.

☐ Mixtures have specific melting and boiling points.

3. **Tick which process applies to each of these sentences.**

	condensation	evaporation
a) Particles need to gain energy for this process to occur.	☐	☐
b) A decrease in temperature causes this process.	☐	☐
c) A liquid becomes a gas.	☐	☐
d) Particles become closer together.	☐	☐
e) Particles need to lose energy for this process to occur.	☐	☐

Filtration and Evaporation

1. Filtration separates solids from liquids. Circle the correct words in this paragraph.

Filtration separates **soluble / insoluble** solid substances from a liquid. A mixture of flour and water can be separated using filter paper. The water particles are small enough to pass through the filter paper — the water is called the **filtrate / residue**. The flour particles are too big to pass through the filter paper so they stay behind — the flour is called the **filtrate / residue**.

2. Evaporation can also be used to separate substances. True or False:

	True	False
a) Evaporation can be used to separate a dissolved solid from a liquid.	☐	☐
b) When liquids evaporate fully into a gas, they decrease in mass.	☐	☐
c) Substances with different boiling points can be separated using evaporation.	☐	☐
d) The liquid that is removed during evaporation can be collected.	☐	☐

3. Ryan collects a beaker full of seawater, sand and pebbles from the beach. He wants to separate the pebbles and sand into different containers, and to remove the water to leave behind any dissolved substances.

PRACTICAL

a) How could he separate the pebbles from the rest of the mixture?

....

....

b) Ryan pours the remaining mixture of sand and seawater through filter paper. Explain how this step works, and say what would be in the residue and the filtrate.

....

....

Residue: .... Filtrate: ....

c) He then uses an evaporating basin and Bunsen burner to heat the filtrate. Explain what happens in this step, and what will be left at the end.

....

....

....

Chromatography

1. Label the chromatography equipment with the words below.

chromatography paper	pencil line	beaker	solvent	ink spot

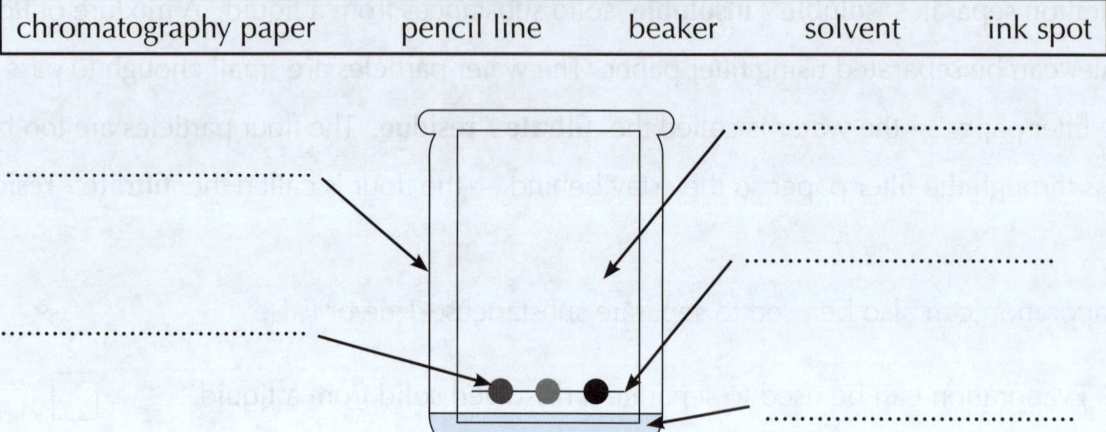

2. Chromatography can be used to separate different coloured substances. It can also be used to help identify unknown substances in a mixture.

a) The spots travel at different speeds. Do they all travel the same distance?

....

b) Phoebe uses three unknown substances to get the chromatography paper shown below. For each statement, say whether she is correct or incorrect and explain why.

i) Substance C is a mixture of substances, one of which could be substance A.

....

....

....

A B C

ii) Substance B must be insoluble, as it hasn't moved very far.

....

....

c) She then says that substance A could be a pure substance. Why do you think she says that?

....

....

....

Chromatography

3. Gary is a crime scene investigator. He finds a message written on the wall at a crime scene, written in blue paint. Three suspects were found nearby, all with blue paint on their clothes.

a) He takes samples of paint from the wall and from the three shirts.
He then uses chromatography to separate the substances in the paints.
The chromatography paper is shown below.

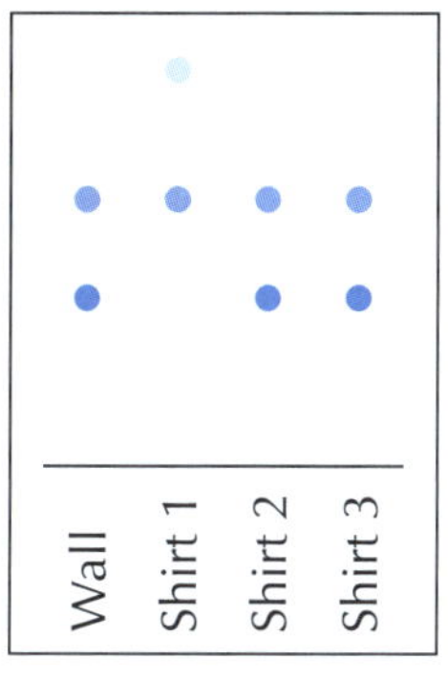

You can try, but you'll never catch me...

Exhibit A: the message

Exhibit B: shirt with paint

i) What can you tell from these results about the total number of substances present in the paints?

....

ii) Which shirt can be ruled out because it doesn't have the same paint as the message? Explain why.

....

....

b) Paint from two of the samples seems to match the paint used for the message.
Gary puts the chromatography paper under a UV lamp, showing a new substance.

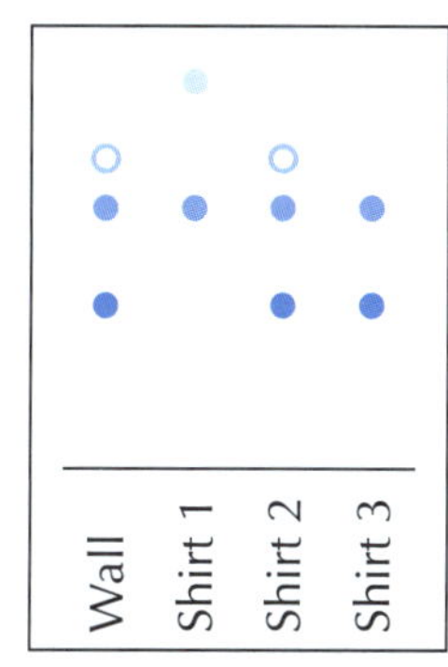

What can you say now about which shirt's paint was used to write the message?

....

....

c) Why does the line the samples start from have to be drawn in pencil and not in pen?

....

Distillation

1. Distillation can be used to separate a liquid from a mixture.

a) What two changes of state take place during distillation?

....

b) What difference in properties is needed to separate two substances by distillation?

....

2. Label the distillation equipment with the words below.

Bunsen burner	clamp stand	condenser	distillate
liquid mixture	boiling flask	thermometer	

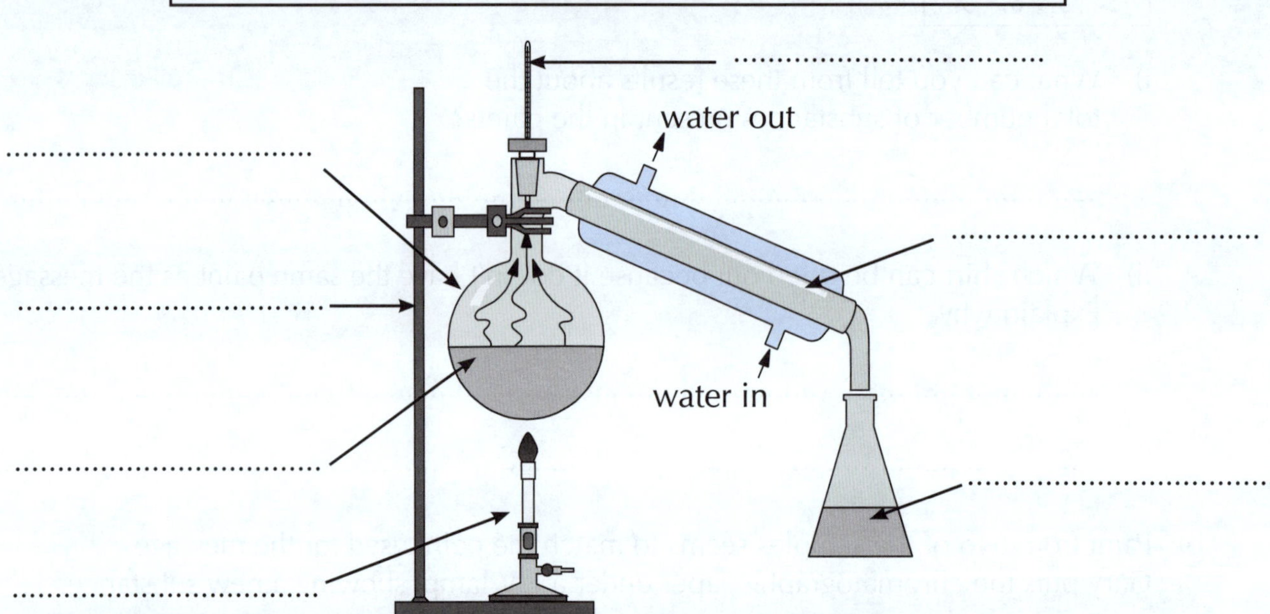

3. Number these steps to give the correct order of the distillation process. The first one has been done for you.

.... Pure water evaporates from the mixture to become water vapour.

.... Water vapour condenses and the water drips into the distillate flask.

1 A mixture of salty water is heated in a boiling flask.

.... Pure water is collected in the distillate flask.

.... The water vapour enters the condenser and cools down.

Distillation

4. Mary works in a lab. She has a mixture of liquid A (boiling point 65 °C), liquid B (boiling point 68 °C) and water that she wants to separate using distillation.

a) She says the first liquid from the condenser will be pure water. Explain why she is wrong.

....

....

b) Explain why she will be able to separate the water from the other two liquids.

....

....

c) Explain why it would be hard to separate liquid A and liquid B using distillation.

....

....

....

d) Fractional distillation can be used to separate more complicated mixtures. The diagram below shows the equipment used in fractional distillation. Gases rise up out of the flask into the fractionating column. The column is hotter at the bottom than at the top.

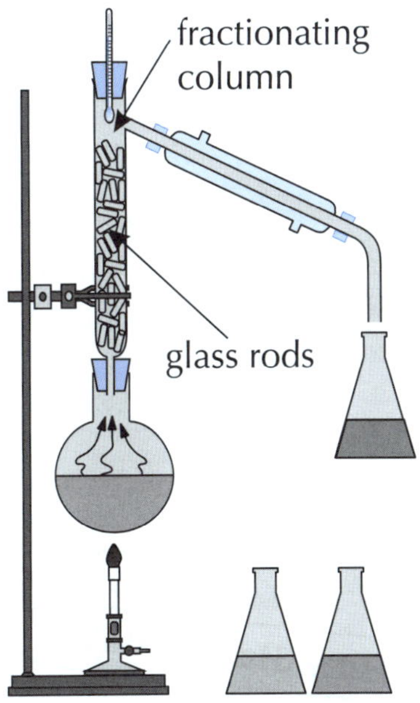

i) Mary uses this equipment to heat another sample of her mixture to 65 °C. What will happen to the different liquids at this temperature?

....

....

....

....

ii) The temperature at the top of the column is 60 °C. What happens to the substances at the top of the column?

....

....

....

....

Distillation

5. Crude oil is a mixture of lots of different substances.
Sometimes, oil spills cause oil to build up on beaches.

a) Levi takes a sample from a beach that is a mixture of crude oil, sand and some seawater. He knows that oil floats on water, and that sand is insoluble in water. Why would adding more water help separate the sand from the rest of the mixture?

....

....

b) Levi decides to carry out fractional distillation on the crude oil and water mixture. The parts of the mixture he collects are called fractions. The fractions are collected in order from lowest to highest boiling point. These are the boiling points for the fractions in the crude oil that he collects:

gasoline: 30-80 °C
kerosene: 200-250 °C
diesel: 250-350 °C

i) He collects four fractions in total. He numbers the fractions from 1 to 4 in the order he collects them. Which fraction is water?

....

ii) Two of the fractions might overlap slightly. Explain which two, and why.

....

....

iii) After the four fractions have come off the column, Levi stops heating the mixture. A thick, black substance is left. He says that this must be a pure substance with a very high boiling point. Explain why he is partly correct.

....

....

....

How did you do?

There are lots of techniques to learn — each one uses a specific property of a substance. You should:

- [ ] Know that the choice of separation method depends on the substances.
- [ ] Understand that chromatography can be used to separate and identify substances.
- [ ] Understand that filtration and evaporation both separate solids from liquids.
- [ ] Know that distillation works because liquids have different boiling points.

Topic 8 — Reactions with Acids and Alkalis

Hopefully this topic gets a reaction out of you — it's pretty exciting (trust me)...

Learning Objectives

1. Understand that particles are rearranged in a chemical reaction.
2. Know the differences between chemical reactions and physical changes.
3. Understand that acids and alkalis react together to form a salt and water in a neutralisation reaction.
4. Know how to name salts formed in neutralisation reactions.

Before you Start

1. **Tick whether these substances are acidic, neutral or alkaline.**

	acidic	neutral	alkaline
a) Indigestion tablet (pH 10)	☐	☐	☐
b) Tomato juice (pH 4.5)	☐	☐	☐
c) Pure water (pH 7)	☐	☐	☐
d) Stomach acid (pH 2)	☐	☐	☐
e) Bleach (pH 13)	☐	☐	☐

2. **Circle the correct words in this paragraph.**

Universal indicator is used to show the **pH / type** of an acid or alkali. Universal indicator turns **blue / green** in a neutral substance. **Acids / Alkalis** have low pH values and turn universal indicator **red / purple**. **Acids / Alkalis** have high pH values and turn universal indicator **red / purple**. Different indicators have different pH ranges.

3. **Tick any reversible changes.**

Baking cake mixture in the oven ☐
Melting butter in a pan ☐
Freezing water in an ice cube tray ☐
Toasting some bread ☐
Boiling water in a kettle ☐
Burning a piece of wood on a fire ☐

Chemical Reactions

1. Chemical reactions are different to physical changes.
Tick which of these statements are true or false.

True False

a) Particles are rearranged in chemical reactions. ☐ ☐

b) Physical changes are usually harder to reverse than chemical reactions. ☐ ☐

2. Word equations show what happens in a reaction.
Complete these word equations.

a) Magnesium sulfide is formed when magnesium is heated with sulfur

.... + ... ⟶ ....
....

b) Calcium oxide and carbon dioxide are formed when calcium carbonate breaks down

.... ⟶ .... + ...
....

c) Zinc nitrate and lead are formed when zinc metal is placed in lead nitrate solution

.... + ... ⟶ .... + ...
....

3. Changes are happening all around us.

a) Iron reacts with oxygen to form iron oxide, which is rust.
Say whether this is a chemical reaction or a physical change, and explain why.

....

....

b) Greg says that dissolving salt in water is an example of a chemical reaction.
Explain why he is incorrect.

....

....

Neutralisation Reactions

1. Circle the correct words in this paragraph.

An alkali is an example of **a soluble / an insoluble** base.

A base is a substance that neutralises an **alkali / acid**.

Neutralisation reactions form a salt and **water / oxygen**.

2. The name of a salt is split into two parts. The second part is taken from the acid used in the neutralisation reaction that makes the salt. Match each acid to the salt formed.

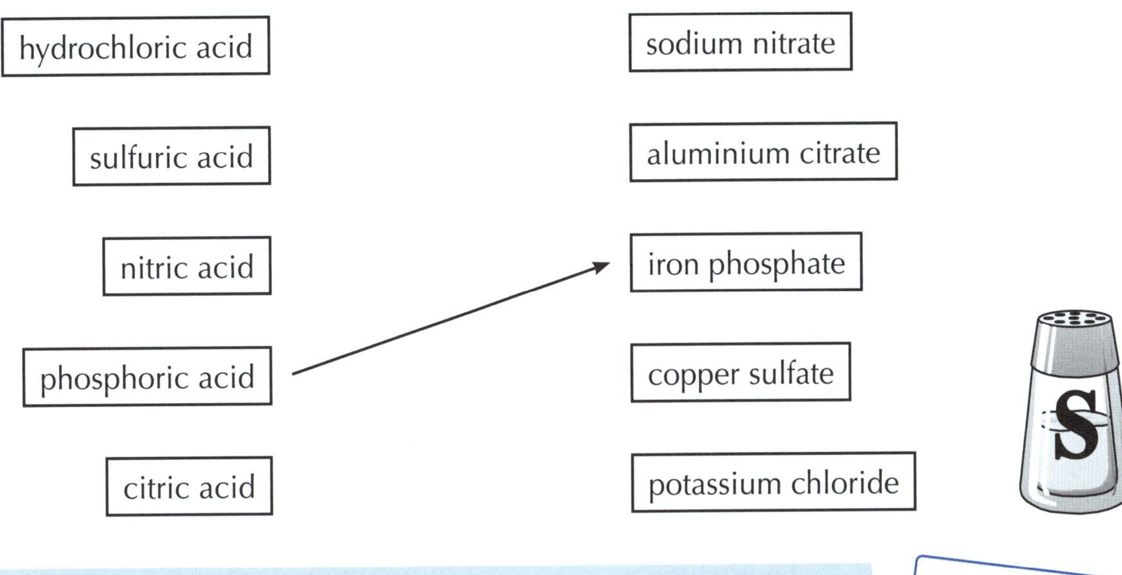

3. Maya is using lithium hydroxide solution to neutralise hydrochloric acid.

a) She mixes the two colourless liquids and the mixture stays colourless. She says that no salt has formed because she can't see it. Explain why she is incorrect.

....

....

b) What is the name of the salt formed during the neutralisation reaction?

....

c) Suggest what she could use to know when the reaction has reached a neutral pH, and say what she would see.

....

d) She accidentally spills some of the acid on the worktop. Explain why using lithium hydroxide could make the acid safe to be cleaned up.

....

....

Neutralisation Reactions

4. The stomach contains stomach acid which allows enzymes to digest food. Acid reflux is when some of the stomach acid moves back into the food pipe. One symptom of acid reflux is heartburn.

a) Antacids are used as treatment for acid reflux, as they neutralise the acid. Suggest what type of substance an antacid is, and how it would help treat acid reflux.

....

....

....

b) Taking too many antacids may make it harder for the stomach to digest food. Why do you think this is?

....

....

c) The acid in the stomach is hydrochloric acid. One example of a substance used in antacids is aluminium hydroxide. Fill in the name of the salt produced in this reaction in the word equation below.

aluminium hydroxide + hydrochloric acid ⟶ .... + water

d) i) Another substance that is often used in antacids is magnesium carbonate. Fill in the name of the salt produced in the word equation below.

magnesium carbonate + hydrochloric acid ⟶ .... + water + carbon dioxide

ii) Walter wants to see what happens when he mixes a spatula of magnesium carbonate powder into a beaker of hydrochloric acid. The solution fizzes as it reacts. What do you think causes this?

....

iii) One of the side effects of using antacids is feeling bloated and gassy. Suggest which antacid (the one with aluminium hydroxide or with magnesium carbonate) would be more likely to cause this side effect, and explain why.

....

....

....

Neutralisation Reactions

5. Old MacDonald has a farm. He is planning what crops to grow for the year. Different crops prefer soil of different pH values. Some information is shown below.

SCIENCE IN ACTION

Potatoes prefer pH 5.5–6.0

Strawberries prefer pH 5.5–7.0

Carrots prefer pH 6.0–7.0

Radishes prefer pH 6.5–7.0

a) He measures the pH value of the soil to be 5.8. What two crops would grow best at this pH value?

....

b) i) He decides to plant carrots and radishes. What pH range would suit both crops best?

....

ii) Agricultural lime is added to soil to increase the soil's pH. Lime is mostly made up of calcium carbonate. Old MacDonald adds lime to the soil and the pH increases to a value of 6.8. Explain what will happen in the soil when lime is added.

....

....

....

6. Bee stings contain a mixture of substances, including some acids. Calamine lotion contains zinc oxide, which is a base.

SCIENCE IN ACTION

a) Explain why calamine lotion could help relieve the pain of the bee sting.

....

....

b) Wasp stings are slightly alkaline. Explain why calamine lotion would not be as useful for relieving wasp stings, and suggest another substance that could be used instead.

....

....

....

How did you do?

It's good to know what happens when you put acids and alkalis together. By now you should:

- [ ] Understand that particles are rearranged in a chemical reaction.
- [ ] Know the differences between chemical and physical changes.
- [ ] Understand that acids and alkalis react together in neutralisation reactions.
- [ ] Know how to name the salts formed in neutralisation reactions.

Topic 9 — Reactions with Metals and Non-Metals

Don't be too surprised, but you're not done with reactions just yet — here's a load more...

Learning Objectives

1. Understand oxidation reactions of metals and non-metals.
2. Know that the reaction between an acid and a metal produces a salt and hydrogen.
3. Know what a displacement reaction is and when they take place.
4. Be able to interpret a reactivity series.
5. Understand how carbon can be used to extract metals from metal oxides.

Before you Start

1. **Circle any substances that are metal.**

gold oxygen sulfur hydrogen silver

mercury titanium fish fingers bromine iron

2. **Which sentences about acids and bases are true?**

- ☐ An acid has a pH of below 7.
- ☐ A neutral substance has a pH of 8.
- ☐ An alkali is a soluble base.
- ☐ Adding water to a base will neutralise it.

3. **Put each situation into the correct column in the table.**

iron turning into rust seawater evaporating to leave salt

sugar dissolving in water vinegar fizzing with baking soda

wood burning on a bonfire ink spreading out in water

Physical Change	Chemical Reaction

4. **Write out the word equation for the reaction between zinc and sulfur to form zinc sulfide.**

....

Oxidation of Metals and Non-Metals

1. Oxidation is a type of reaction. Tick a box for each sentence to show whether it is true or false.

	True	False
a) Oxidation reactions are when substances combine with carbon.	☐	☐
b) Metals and non-metals can both react in oxidation reactions.	☐	☐
c) Non-metal oxides usually have a neutral pH.	☐	☐

2. Lithium is a metal.

a) Write out the word equation for when lithium burns.

.... + ... ⟶ ....

b) The substance formed in this reaction dissolves in water. Predict the pH of this solution. Circle the correct answer.

Less than 7 **7** **More than 7**

3. Lithium and potassium are both metals that have to be stored in oil. Savannah wants to know which metal oxidises quicker.

a) She takes a piece of each metal out of the oil. They are both shiny. After a few seconds, the potassium turns dull. The lithium turns a dull grey colour after a minute. Which metal oxidised more easily?

....

b) Savannah and Mike are discussing different oxidation reactions.

Savannah: When iron is oxidised it becomes iron oxide, which is known as rust.

Mike: Copper can also rust because it changes colour when you leave it for a long time.

i) Savannah is correct, but Mike is not. What could Savannah say to correct Mike?

....

....

ii) They both agree that iron and copper react less easily than lithium and potassium. How do they know?

....

....

Metals and Acids

1. Some metals react with acids to produce a salt and a gas.

a) What would you expect to see happening in a metal-acid reaction that wouldn't happen in the reaction of an alkali and an acid?

....

b) What gas is produced when a metal reacts with an acid?

☐ oxygen ☐ carbon dioxide ☐ hydrogen

c) Write down the names of the salts produced in these reactions of metals with acids.

i) calcium + sulfuric acid ....

ii) lead + nitric acid ....

2. Barnaby is investigating how different metals react with dilute nitric acid.

a) He adds samples of magnesium, tin, gold and zinc to separate beakers of the acid and collects the gas produced for each reaction.
He observes the reactions and records what he sees in the table below.

Metal	Description of Reaction
magnesium	very rapid bubbling
tin	very slow bubbling
gold	no bubbling
zinc	slow bubbling at first, then rapid bubbling

i) Which metal reacted the fastest? ....

ii) Which metal reacted the least? ....

b) Barnaby says that tin and zinc are equally reactive, because both bubbled slowly to start with. Explain why he is incorrect, and say which of the two metals is more reactive.

....

....

c) Write out the word equation for the reaction between magnesium and dilute nitric acid.

.... + ... → .... + ...

....

Displacement Reactions

1. Circle the correct words in this paragraph.

A displacement reaction is a reaction where a **more / less** reactive metal takes the place of a **more / less** reactive metal in a substance. Displacement reactions can be used to work out which metals are the **strongest / most reactive**.

2. Displacement reactions can happen when you put a metal into a solution of a different metal salt. An iron nail is placed into a solution of copper sulfate, which is blue.

a) A brown coating appears on the outside of the nail. What do you think this is?

....

b) The solution turns a green colour. What do you think has happened?

....

....

c) Write out the word equation for this displacement reaction.

.... + ... → .... + ...

3. Some car air bags contain sodium azide, which is a substance made from sodium. During an impact, the sodium azide is heated and breaks down to produce sodium metal and nitrogen gas, which inflates the air bag.

SCIENCE IN ACTION

a) Sodium azide breaks down at 275 °C. Potassium azide is made from potassium and breaks down at 355 °C. Why do you think it is better to use sodium azide in an air bag?

....

....

b) Sodium metal is very reactive. Potassium is more reactive than sodium. Suggest another reason why sodium azide is used instead of potassium azide.

....

....

c) These air bags also contain iron oxide, which reacts with the sodium that is made. Write out the word equation for this displacement reaction.

.... + ... → .... + ...

Displacement Reactions

4. Elijah is investigating how reactive strips of magnesium, copper, lead and zinc are. He carries out four different displacement reactions.

Reaction	Metal	Salt Solution	Reaction?
1	magnesium	copper sulfate	yes
2	magnesium	zinc sulfate	yes
3	lead	copper sulfate	yes
4	zinc	lead nitrate	yes

a) After a while, the solution in reaction 1 turns from blue to colourless, and a brown substance coats the magnesium strip.

i) Elijah says that magnesium is more reactive than copper. Explain why he is right.

....

....

ii) Write out the word equation for this reaction.

.... + ... ⟶ .... + ...

b) Elijah thinks that copper is less reactive than zinc.
Suggest another reaction that he could carry out to confirm this.

....

....

c) List the metals (magnesium, copper, lead, zinc) in order of how reactive they are.

.... *most reactive*

....

....

.... *least reactive*

d) Elijah's teacher wants him to add silver to his reactivity series. She says that silver is less reactive than magnesium, copper, lead and zinc. How can he show with just one more reaction that silver is less reactive than the other metals?

....

....

The Reactivity Series and Extraction

1. Circle the correct words to complete this paragraph on reactivity.

Reactivity is how likely a substance is to go through a **physical / chemical** change.

The more reactive something is, the **more / less** likely it is to react.

A reactivity series is a list of **substances / salts** in order of their reactivity.

You can use a reactivity series to predict whether a reaction is likely to happen.

2. Using the reactivity series below, predict whether these reactions would take place or not.

	yes	no
a) strontium + titanium chloride	☐	☐
b) cadmium + strontium chloride	☐	☐
c) beryllium + bismuth chloride	☐	☐
d) bismuth + cadmium chloride	☐	☐
e) titanium + beryllium fluoride	☐	☐

Strontium *most reactive*
Beryllium
Titanium
Cadmium
Bismuth *least reactive*

3. Owen has two unknown metals, X and Y. They fit in the spaces shown in his reactivity series below, but he is unsure which way round they go.

Potassium *most reactive*
....
Calcium
Magnesium
Zinc
....
Copper *least reactive*

a) Both metals react with acids. Using the reactivity series, describe how the two reactions would be different.

....

....

....

....

....

....

b) Only Y reacts with water. Put X and Y into the correct positions on the reactivity series.

c) Owen says that both metals X and Y would react with copper chloride solution. Explain why he is correct.

....

....

The Reactivity Series and Extraction

4. Metals are often mined as ores which contain metal oxides. Some metals can be extracted from metal oxides using carbon.

a) Carbon reacts with the metal oxide to form carbon dioxide and the metal. Finish the word equations for two of these extraction reactions.

i) copper oxide + ... → .... + carbon dioxide

ii) .... + ... → iron + ...

b) Aluminium is above carbon in the reactivity series. Explain why the aluminium in aluminium oxide cannot be extracted using carbon.

....

....

5. Helena is investigating the reactivity of iron, silver and calcium. She adds a piece of each metal to separate beakers of dilute hydrochloric acid. Her data is shown in the table below.

Metal	Description of Reaction
iron	slow bubbling
silver	no bubbling
calcium	very rapid bubbling

a) List the three metals in order of their reactivity, starting with the most reactive.

....

b) Helena adds an iron nail to a solution of silver nitrate. Will a reaction occur?

☐ yes ☐ no

c) Helena adds an iron nail to a calcium chloride solution. Explain why nothing happens.

....

....

d) Helena predicts that if she adds calcium to iron sulfate solution, a reaction will take place. Explain why she is correct.

....

....

The Reactivity Series and Extraction

6. Different metals are used to make different containers.

SCIENCE IN ACTION

a) Lead is often used to line containers that hold radioactive material. Using your knowledge of the reactivity series, explain what would happen if you tried to store a copper nitrate solution in a lead-lined container.

b) Drinks cans can be made of aluminium or tinplate (steel coated with tin). Neither aluminium nor tin react with water, but aluminium can react with steam.

i) Based on reactivity, explain if aluminium or tinplate is better to use in drinks cans.

When aluminium reacts with oxygen in air, it produces aluminium oxide, which sticks to the aluminium. Aluminium oxide is very unreactive.

ii) Why might it be useful to have a layer of aluminium oxide on an aluminium can?

Tin was first extracted from its ore using carbon around 5000 years ago. Aluminium ores have been used by humans for at least 2500 years, but pure aluminium was not extracted from its ore until around 200 years ago.

iii) Aluminium is more reactive than carbon. Use this fact to explain why tin has been used by humans for longer than pure aluminium.

c) Iron can be protected from rusting by coating it in a thin layer of zinc in a process called galvanisation. The zinc layer is oxidised instead of the iron. Write out word equations for the oxidation reactions of both iron and zinc.

Iron: ....

Zinc: ....

The Reactivity Series and Extraction

7. Alfie is using displacement reactions to predict rates of oxidation for different metals. His data is shown in the table below.

Metal	Salt Solution	Displacement?
cobalt	calcium chloride	no
calcium	gold nitrate	yes
gold	cobalt chloride	no

a) Which metal would react with oxygen the quickest? ....

b) Write out the word equation for the reaction of cobalt with oxygen.

.... + ... ⟶ ....

c) Explain how the information above shows a property of gold that makes it a good material for using in jewellery.

....

....

d) Alfie has the results from three more displacement reactions. Use all six reactions to create a reactivity series for the five metals (cobalt, calcium, gold, silver and copper).

Metal	Salt Solution	Displacement?
silver	gold nitrate	yes
copper	cobalt chloride	no
copper	silver nitrate	yes

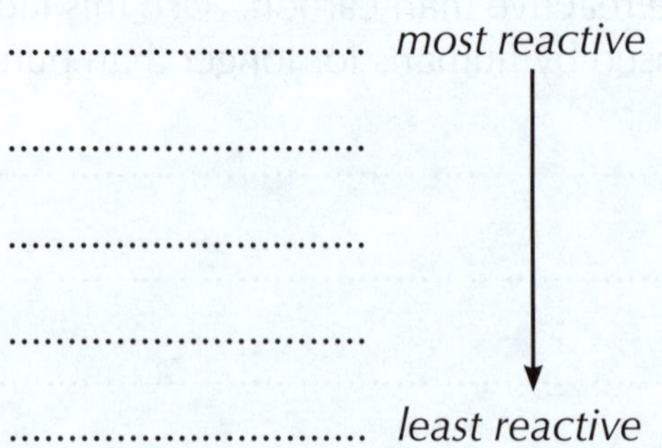

e) Sterling silver is a mixture of the metals silver and copper. It is used to make jewellery. Sometimes sterling silver causes green staining on skin. Which metal do you think is responsible for this? Explain why.

....

....

The Reactivity Series and Extraction

8. Harriet wants to create a reactivity series for five metals — manganese, gold, mercury, barium and nickel. Some information is available for each metal.

Ore Extraction

Gold: often exists as a pure metal

Mercury: extracted from its ore using heat

Barium: cannot be extracted using carbon or heat

Reactions with Water

Manganese does not react with water, but does react with steam.

Nickel does not react with water or steam.

Reactions with Acids

Nickel and manganese both produce bubbles when placed in hydrochloric acid.

Mercury does not produce any bubbles in hydrochloric acid.

Oxidation

Barium oxidises quickly in air.

Gold does not oxidise in air.

Manganese reacts with air when heated.

a) Using all of the information shown, complete the reactivity series below and explain why you have put the substances in that order.

.... *most reactive*

....

....

....

.... *least reactive*

....

....

....

....

....

....

....

....

b) Harriet finds out that manganese is extracted using carbon. Where would carbon fit in your reactivity series?

....

How did you do?

You'll be relieved to know that's it for reactions for now. By now, you should be happy that you:

- ☐ Understand oxidation reactions of metals and non-metals.
- ☐ Know that an acid and metal react to produce a salt and hydrogen.
- ☐ Know what a displacement reaction is and when they take place.
- ☐ Be able to interpret a reactivity series and understand how carbon can extract metals.

Topic 10 — The Universe

If this dot • is the Earth, then the Sun is the size of a grapefruit 11 m away (the length of a bus). Woah...

Learning Objectives

1. Know about our solar system and what we can see in the night sky.
2. Understand why we have seasons.
3. Understand why an object's weight is different on different planets.
4. Know how gravity affects planets, moons and stars.
5. Know what stars, solar systems and galaxies are.

Before you Start

1. **Are the statements below about gravity and mass true or false? Tick the correct answer.**

	True	False
Everything with mass has gravity.	☐	☐
The less mass something has, the stronger its gravity.	☐	☐
Weight is the same thing as mass.	☐	☐
The closer objects are together, the stronger the gravity is between them.	☐	☐

2. **The diagram below shows the Sun, the Earth and the Moon. Draw circles on the diagram to show their orbits.**

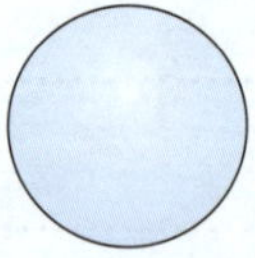

Not drawn to scale

3. **Select the correct word from each pair to complete the sentences below.**

The Moon is a rocky **sphere / cube** that orbits the **Earth / Solar System.**

It is a natural **trampoline / satellite.**

The Moon's orbit takes about a **week / month.**

The Moon is bright because it **gives out / reflects** light.

The Solar System

1. The diagram below shows the planets in our solar system.

Complete the diagram by labelling the planets. Two have already been done for you.

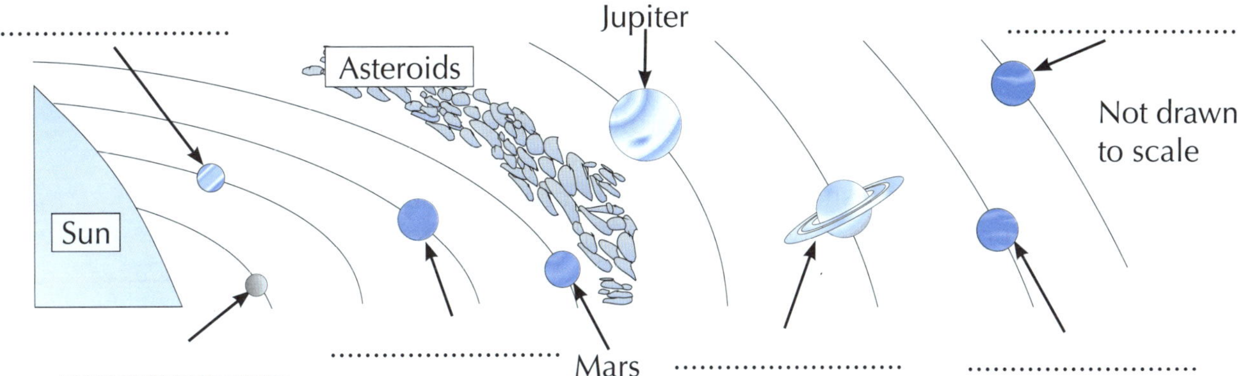

2. The diagram on the right shows four planets in our solar system. Nicolaus is on Earth at the point marked with an arrow. He looks into the night sky.

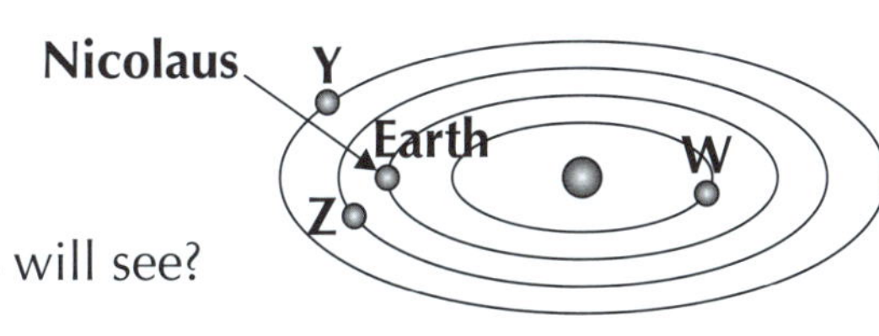

a) Which diagram below could show what Nicolaus will see? Circle the correct answer.

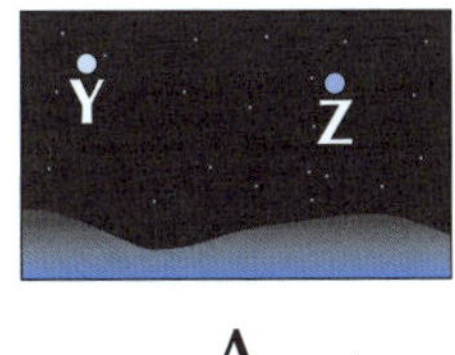

A

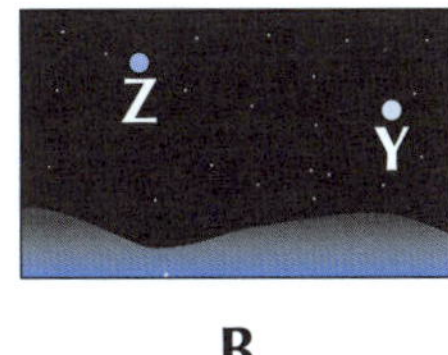

B

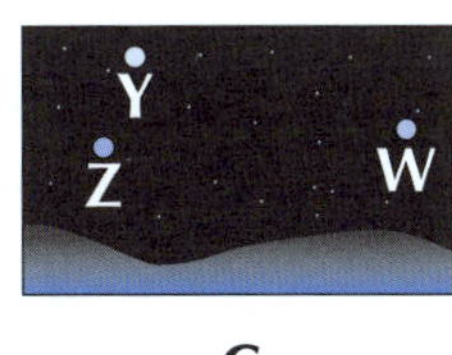

C

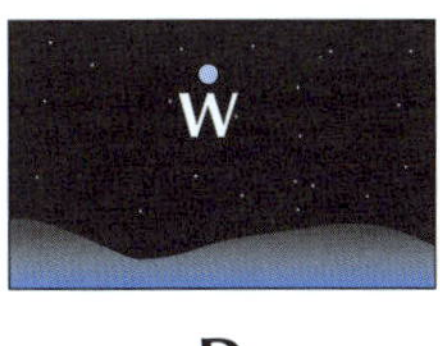

D

b) Explain how the way the solar system is arranged allows Nicolaus to see the planets in the night sky.

....

....

c) Nicolaus knows there may be exoplanets much further away that he can't see. What is an exoplanet?

....

3. Ancient people thought that the planets, the Moon and the Sun all orbited the Earth.

a) Why do you think watching the Sun throughout the day would lead ancient people to believe this?

....

....

The Solar System

b) Looking from Earth, some planets appear to move in one direction and then backward in the other direction. Explain how this shows the planets do not orbit the Earth.

....

....

4. The Earth rotates on a tilted axis as it orbits the sun.

a) The diagram below shows how the Earth orbits the Sun. In each box write the season (summer or winter) that it will be in the northern hemisphere.

North Pole

Sun

South Pole

b) What season is it in the southern hemisphere if it is winter in the UK?

....

c) Why are there fewer daylight hours in the winter than in the summer in the UK?

....

....

....

d) Kuala Lumpur is the capital of Malaysia. It is near the equator. What do you think happens to the number of daylight hours in Kuala Lumpur as the Earth orbits the Sun?

....

e) Helle's teacher asks Helle why it is warmer in the UK in summer than it is in winter.

Helle: It must be because in the summer there are more hours of sunlight.

Teacher: That's one reason, but it doesn't fully explain the difference. In summer the UK has much longer days than warmer countries closer to the equator.

Explain the other reason the UK is warmer in summer than in winter.

....

....

....

The Solar System

5. Ziggog is a space kangaroo. She is planning to visit some new planets.

a) Ziggog has a mass of 75 kg. Fill in the table below with Ziggog's weight on different planets. The first one has been done for you.

Planet	Gravitational strength (N/kg)	Ziggog's weight (N)
Hecate	2	150
Singe	17.1	
Turtle	5	
Osiris	6.9	
Elatha	22.5	

Ziggog only wants to visit planets where she can jump.
She calculates that she can jump as long as her weight is less than 500 N.

b) i) Which of these planets should Ziggog visit?

....

ii) On which of these planets will Ziggog be able to jump the highest?

....

c) All of the planets in the table have the same diameter.
Which of the planets do you think has the largest mass? Why do you think this?

....

....

Planet Osiris has two moons, Rha and Horus. Both moons have the same mass.
Rha is 240 000 km from Osiris. Horus is 400 000 km from Osiris.

d) Ziggog thinks that the gravitational force will be stronger between Osiris and Horus than it will be between Osiris and Rha. Do you agree with Ziggog, and why?

....

....

Stars and Galaxies and the Universe

1. Each of the following statements is incorrect. Keeping the words in bold, write correct versions of each statement underneath.

a) **A star is** anything in space that we can see.

....

b) **A galaxy is** a star with planets orbiting around it.

....

c) **The Milky Way** is the closest galaxy to **our galaxy**.

....

2. Answer the following questions about light years.

a) i) What is a light year?

....

....

ii) Why do we measure distances in space using light years instead of km?

....

....

b) It takes around 1.3 seconds for light from the Moon to reach the Earth.

i) How far is the Moon from the Earth in light seconds?

....

ii) On average, the Moon is about 380 000 km from the Earth. Use this to say which is larger — one light second or one km.

380 000 km is equal to your answer in part i.

....

c) The Sun is about 150 000 000 km from Earth. Which of the following do you think is the distance between the Sun and the Earth? Circle the correct answer.

8 light seconds **8 light minutes** **8 light years** **80 light years**

Stars and Galaxies and the Universe

SCIENCE IN ACTION

3. The closest star to our solar system is Proxima Centauri, at 4.2 light years from Earth.

a) Which of the following statements is correct? Tick the correct box.

- ☐ We see Proxima Centauri as it is right now.
- ☐ We see Proxima Centauri as it was 4.2 years ago.
- ☐ We see Proxima Centauri as it was 42 years ago.
- ☐ We see Proxima Centauri as it will be 4.2 years in the future.

WELCOME HUMANS

b) The greatest speed reached by a spacecraft directly after launch from Earth is about 58 000 km/h. It would take a spacecraft travelling at this speed 18 500 years to travel 1 light year.

MATHS SKILLS

i) How long would it take to reach Proxima Centauri travelling at this speed?

.... years

ii) Why does this make it difficult for humans to travel between solar systems?

....

....

c) In 2018, scientists observed the furthest star that has ever been seen, using the Hubble telescope. The star is 14.4 billion light years away.

i) Why does looking at distant stars help us to understand the history of the universe?

....

....

ii) Our Sun is about 4.6 billion years old. Why would it be impossible for us to see a star formed at the same time as our Sun if it was as far away as the furthest star found by the Hubble telescope?

....

....

How did you do?

The universe is so big, you'd think that there's probably life out there somewhere. Maybe they'll look like us, maybe like a big green blob, maybe even like my cat Steve. By now, you should:

- ☐ Know about our solar system.
- ☐ Understand why we have seasons.
- ☐ Know how gravity affects planets and stars.
- ☐ Know about stars, solar systems and galaxies.

☐ ☐ ☐

Topic 11 — Movement

This is one for your dog — it's full of bones. Oh and some meaty muscle thrown in for good measure.

Learning Objectives

1. Know the four main functions of the human skeleton.
2. Understand how the structure of the skeleton makes it suited to its function.
3. Know that muscles create movement and know what antagonistic muscles are.
4. Understand how the skeleton and muscles interact to move the body.

Before you Start

1. **Which of these animals do you think has a skeleton? Tick the correct box(es).**

☐ ☐ ☐ ☐

2. **Tick the parts of the body below that are not part of the skeleton.**

☐ skull ☐ toenails ☐ tongue ☐ knee caps

3. **Which of the following describe a role of the skeleton? Tick yes or no for each one.**

	Yes	No
a) To supply the body with oxygen.	☐	☐
b) To allow movement of the body.	☐	☐
c) To support the body.	☐	☐
d) To transport substances around the body.	☐	☐
e) To help protect the body's organs.	☐	☐

4. **Circle the correct words to complete the sentences below.**

Bones work together with **muscles** / **the skin** to make the body move. For this movement to happen, **friction** / **a force** must be applied to the skeleton.

The Skeletal System

1. Circle the correct word to complete the sentences below.

a) A strong cord that connects bone to bone is called a **ligament** / **tendon**.

b) A strong cord that connects muscle to bone is called a **ligament** / **tendon**.

2. Below is a diagram of the lower part of a human skeleton.

a) Correctly label one other bone on the diagram.
Choose a name from the box below.

femur	metatarsal	Barry	patella

pelvis

hip joint

b) What is the function of the hip joint?

....

c) The pelvis is needed for protection.

i) Suggest one organ that the pelvis protects.

....

ii) Explain why the physical properties of bone make it good for protection.

....

....

3. Aisha is trying to make a model of a bone. She puts some jelly inside a plastic pipe.

a) Give two physical properties that the model has that makes it similar to real bone.

1. ....

2. ....

plastic pipe

jelly

b) i) What is the name of the substance that the jelly in Aisha's model represents?

....

ii) What is the role of this part in real bone?

....

The Skeletal System

4. Leo is putting up a tent in his garden.
He decides that tent poles are just like the human skeleton.

a) Suggest one function that the skeleton and the tent poles share.
Explain how they share this function.

....

....

....

b) How far do you agree with Leo that, 'tent poles are just like the human skeleton'?

....

....

....

5. Frank has Paget's disease, which affects the bones in his legs.
The disease means his bones are softer than they should be.
The condition has also led to him having osteoarthritis in his knees. Osteoarthritis causes cartilage at joints to break down.

Having Paget's disease has affected the normal functioning of Frank's skeleton.
Complete the table below to suggest why the condition has affected the skeleton's functions of support and movement, and suggest how this might affect Frank's day-to-day life.

Function	Why has it been affected?	How might this affect day-to-day life?
Support		
Movement		

The Muscular System

1. Some muscles in the body are not connected to bones to move the skeleton. The heart is an organ of the body that contains muscle tissue.

a) Use words from the box below to complete the sentences that follow.

contraction	stretches	relaxes	movement	relaxation	stretching	contracts

The .... and ....

of muscle allow it to create .... in the body.

In the heart, when muscle in the walls ....,

it pushes blood out of the heart.

b) Suggest one other organ of the body that contains muscle tissue and suggest the role of muscle in that organ.

....

....

2. Sophia dissected a chicken wing. She drew the diagram below to show what she saw.

a) What is the name of the structure that attaches the biceps to the radius?

....

b) The biceps and triceps muscles are examples of antagonistic muscles. Explain what is meant by the term 'antagonistic muscles'.

....

....

c) Explain how a chicken's muscles make its radius and ulna move up and down.

....

....

....

The Muscular System

3. Edie asked six friends to hold a weight at a 90° angle, as shown below. She then timed how long they could keep the weight in that position. Her results are shown in the table on the right.

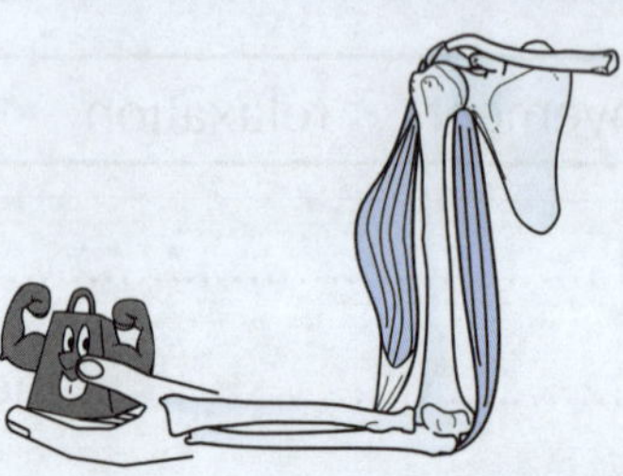

Friend	Time (s)
Laura	13.0
Bella	30.3
Muhammad	32.5
Yohan	40.7
Sara	22.6
Paul	29.5

a) Calculate the mean time the friends held the weight.

MATHS SKILLS

.... s

b) What was the dependent variable in Edie's investigation?

....

c) i) Name two things that are applying a force to the bones in the arm in this experiment.

1. .... 2. ....

ii) What could Edie use to measure the size of the force being applied to the arm?

....

d) After looking at her results, Edie concluded that boys are able to hold weights out at a 90° angle for longer than girls. Give one reason why this is not a valid conclusion.

....

e) Edie repeated the experiment with a much heavier weight, but some of her friends weren't even able to hold the weight at 90° for a second. Suggest an explanation for this.

....

....

....

How did you do?

Your biceps and triceps have been working hard writing all those answers. By now you should:

- ☐ **Know the functions of the human skeleton.**
- ☐ **Know how the structure of the skeleton relates to its functions.**
- ☐ **Know muscles are needed for movement.**
- ☐ **Understand how the skeleton and muscles move the body, including how antagonistic muscles work.**

Topic 12 — Digestion

Have a go at digesting this. Not as tasty as a pizza but it could be described as food for the brain.

Learning Objectives

1. Know that the body needs a balanced diet for energy, growth and maintenance.
2. Know why the body needs each component of a healthy diet.
3. Be able to calculate the energy requirements for a healthy diet.
4. Know some of the possible health effects of an unbalanced diet.
5. Know the role of the digestive system and how the organs it contains are adapted for their functions.
6. Know the role of enzymes in digestion.
7. Know the importance of bacteria in the digestive system.

Before you Start

1. **Tick the true sentence below about human nutrition.**

- [ ] Cells can make their own food.
- [ ] People need to eat the right types of food.
- [ ] All people need the same amount of food.
- [ ] People should avoid eating fats.

2. **Put the following organs in order that food passes through them. Write the numbers 1-4 in the boxes below.**

A  ☐

B 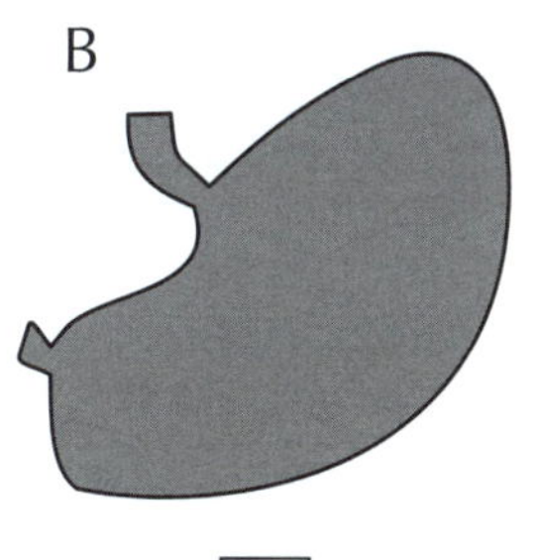 ☐

C 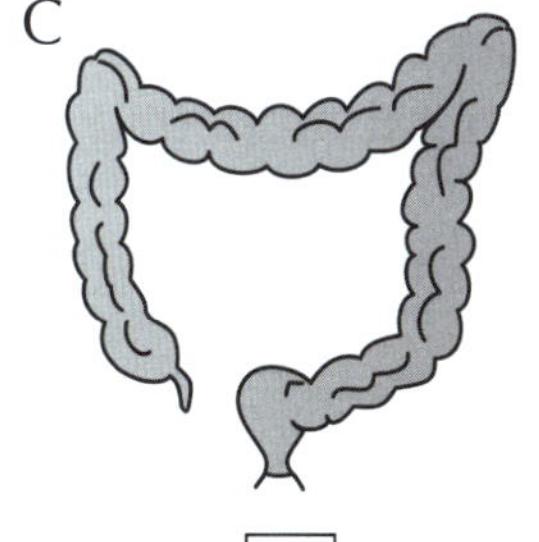 ☐

D 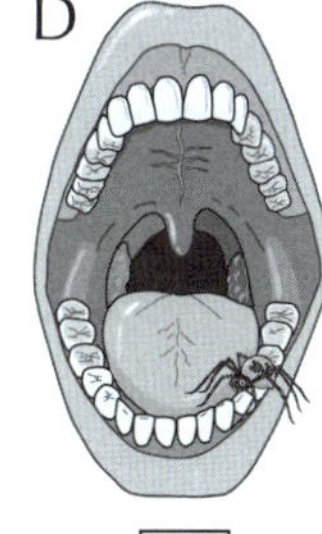 ☐

3. **Draw lines to match the organs in the digestive system with their roles.**

stomach	tears food into bits for swallowing
large intestine	absorbs water into the body
mouth	churns food to help break it down
small intestine	absorbs nutrients into the blood

Nutrition

1. Lipids (fats and oils) are one component of a healthy diet.

a) Circle the foods below that are good sources of lipids.

butter bananas nuts pasta lettuce milk

b) Which of the following statements about lipids is true? Tick the correct box.

☐ They are used to build new tissue. ☐ They help the body to eliminate waste. ☐ They are used as a source of energy.

2. Anil is considering the nutritional qualities of a potato. Use words from the box to fill in the gaps below.

I have many qualities.

slowly	simple	fibre	quickly	obesity	small	protein	complex	dehydration

A potato is about 80% water. Humans need water in their diet to stay healthy and prevent .... Potatoes are a good source of B vitamins, which humans need in .... amounts to stay healthy. The skin of a potato contains more substances that can't be digested than the flesh, suggesting that the skin is a better source of .... Potatoes contain lots of starch, meaning they're a good source of .... carbohydrate.

3. A balanced diet includes vitamins and minerals. Some food products have vitamins and minerals added to them, such as iron and calcium.

a) What is meant by the term 'balanced diet'?

....

b) Why is iron an important mineral in the body?

....

c) Many people choose to drink soya milk as an alternative to cow's milk. Soya milk doesn't naturally contain calcium. Suggest why it may be important for someone who doesn't drink cow's milk to drink soya milk with added calcium.

....

....

....

....

Nutrition

4. Lu kept a food diary for four days. Her diary entries are shown in the table below.

	Breakfast	**Lunch**	**Dinner**
Monday	cereal and milk	pizza	fish and chips
Tuesday	glass of milk	salmon in herb sauce	gammon and egg
Wednesday	camel kebab	chicken nuggets and chips	macaroni cheese
Thursday	wholemeal toast and jam	sausage roll	lasagne and peas

a) Thursday's breakfast is high in carbohydrates.

i) Why are carbohydrates important for the body?

....

ii) There are two types of carbohydrates.
Does Thursday's breakfast contain both types? Explain your answer.

....

....

b) Tuesday's meals are not very balanced.

i) Which nutrient type is the main component of Tuesday's meals?

....

ii) Why is this nutrient important for the body?

....

iii) Give two components of a balanced diet that Lu is lacking on Tuesday.

1. .... 2. ....

c) Lu is constipated. Her friend Mal says that she might not be eating enough fibre.

i) How could a lack of fibre cause constipation?

....

....

ii) Do you agree with Mal that Lu isn't eating enough fibre? Explain your answer.

....

....

Diet

1. Freya is a long distance runner. She weighs 57 kg.

MATHS SKILLS

a) What is her daily basic energy requirement?
Use the formula: Daily BER (kJ/day) = 5.4 × 24 hours × body mass (kg)

.... kJ/day

b) Every day Freya runs for 90 minutes.
A 57 kg person uses about 2900 kJ running for an hour.
Work out the total amount of energy she needs in one day.

Use your answer from part a) in your calculation.

.... kJ/day

2. Gary is a 50-year-old man who requires 10 500 kJ per day.

MATHS SKILLS

a) 20% of this energy should come from protein.
Calculate how much energy should come from protein in kJ.

.... kJ

b) Due to illness, Gary had a long period where he didn't eat much. He was only getting about 7600 kJ a day. His doctor was concerned about the effect that this could have on his health. Give two negative health effects that Gary could have faced from eating very little food.

1. ....

2. ....

c) In particular, the doctor was concerned that Gary wasn't getting enough protein. Gary is a vegan, meaning he doesn't eat any animal-derived foods, such as meat, eggs or dairy products. Suggest two sources of protein Gary could eat.

1. ....

2. ....

d) If a person gets very little protein in their diet for a prolonged period of time, they're at risk of developing a deficiency disease called Kwashiorkor. Which of the following are also examples of deficiency diseases? Tick the correct box(es).

☐ scurvy ☐ iron deficiency anaemia

☐ obesity ☐ heart disease

Diet

3. Levels of obesity in the UK are increasing.

a) Explain how an unbalanced diet can lead to obesity.

....

....

....

b) Give two examples of health problems that are linked to obesity.

1. ....

2. ....

c) Read the newspaper article below.

NEW DIET HELPS TO TACKLE OBESITY

The 'you juice, you lose' diet is claiming to help obese people lose excess weight with an easy to follow plan. The diet involves blending vegetables and fruit to make juices, and drinking one glass of juice instead of meals several times a week. Amanda has been on the diet for a month now and is pleased with her weight loss. She stated, 'I'm so happy to have lost weight. I'm finding the diet pretty easy and I think it's healthy too.'

The company behind the diet are claiming that replacing some meals with just fruit and vegetables means the body becomes healthier. Medical professionals, however, are not happy with the widespread marketing of this diet. Dr Smith said, 'While we encourage people to watch their weight and take steps to lose excess weight, this needs to be done in a healthy way. Fad diets, such as this, could actually be harmful to the body and lead to more problems long term.' Article continued inside.

Discuss whether you agree with the claim that the diet will make obese people healthier.

....

....

....

....

....

....

....

The Digestive System

1. Cells in the body need to use the nutrients in food so that life processes can continue.

Explain why it's important for humans to have a digestive system in order to keep life processes happening.

....

....

....

2. Susi was diagnosed with stomach cancer and had a complete gastrectomy as part of her treatment. This meant her stomach was completely removed, and the lower part of her oesophagus was attached to the top of her small intestine.

a) Which of the following statements is not describing something that normally happens in the stomach? Tick the correct sentence.

☐ Food is mixed with acidic juices. ☐ Microorganisms are killed.

☐ Water is absorbed into the blood. ☐ Proteins begin to get broken down.

b) The stomach contains lots of muscular tissue. Explain how this adaptation aids digestion.

....

....

c) After her complete gastrectomy, Susi still eats many of the same foods that she ate before the operation. However, she was advised just to eat small meals.

i) Suggest why Susi was advised to eat small meals following her complete gastrectomy.

....

ii) When food enters Susi's small intestine, it's still partially digested. Explain why.

....

....

....

iii) Describe what happens to the food matter in Susi's digestive system once it has passed through her small intestine.

....

....

....

The Digestive System

3. Bailey is discussing bacteria in the digestive system with his friend Annabel.

Bailey: Did you know that there are bacteria in our digestive systems that help us to break down food?

Annabel: Ha ha ha — oh Bailey, that can't be right because bacteria make us really ill if they get into our bodies. Also, the acid in the stomach would destroy the bacteria.

a) Suggest what Bailey's reply might be to help Annabel understand why both statements she made are incorrect.

b) Describe one way in which bacteria help us digest food.

4. The small intestine has an important role to play in digestion.

a) Enzymes are secreted into the small intestine. Describe the role of enzymes in digestion.

villi

blood vessels

b) The diagram on the right shows part of the inner surface of the small intestine.

i) The small intestine has a good blood supply. Explain why this is important.

ii) Coeliac disease is a disorder in which the villi can appear flattened. Suggest why people with this disease may be at risk of not getting enough nutrients.

SCIENCE IN ACTION

The Digestive System

5. Finn has made a model of a small intestine using Visking tubing. Visking tubing has tiny holes in it that let small molecules through but not bigger ones.

PRACTICAL

He conducted an experiment to investigate the breakdown of starch by amylase. Amylase is an enzyme found in the digestive system, which helps to break down starch molecules into smaller, sugar molecules. This is the method he used:

1. Put some starch solution and amylase solution into some Visking tubing (the tubing needs to be tied at both ends).
2. Put the Visking tubing into a boiling tube of water.
3. Wait for 30 minutes.
4. Take a sample of the liquid outside the Visking tubing and test how much sugar it contains.

Visking tubing

starch solution and amylase solution

water

a) There is sugar in the water outside the Visking tubing at the end of the experiment, but not at the start. Explain why this is.

....

....

b) Give two reasons why Finn's experiment is a good way to model the small intestine.

1. ....

2. ....

c) Finn plans to repeat the experiment but change the concentration of amylase solution he uses, to test how this affects the results. Give two variables he should keep the same each time he repeats the experiment.

1. ....

2. ....

How did you do?

You've finished all the questions on digestion and now you can put your digestive system to good use by eating that biscuit. Go on, you deserve it. By now you should:

- [ ] Know why the body needs a balanced diet.
- [ ] Know the importance of each component of a healthy diet.
- [ ] Be able to carry out calculations of energy requirements for a healthy diet.
- [ ] Know some possible health effects of an unbalanced diet.
- [ ] Understand the role of the digestive system.
- [ ] Know how organs of the digestive system are adapted for their function.
- [ ] Know that enzymes speed up digestion.
- [ ] Understand why bacteria are important for digestion.

Topic 13 — Plant Reproduction

There's a sweet scent in the air — here's a topic all about flowers and plant reproduction.

Learning Objectives

1. Know the structure of a flower and how each part is used in plant reproduction.
2. Know about pollination and how it can lead to fertilisation.
3. Know how plants are adapted for different types of pollination.
4. Understand how seeds form and know about seed dispersal.

Before you Start

1. **What is a fruit? Tick one box.**

☐ Something that makes food for a plant.

☐ Something that contains seeds.

☐ Something that tempts insects to pollinate a plant.

2. **Fill in the missing words in the sentences below using these options.**

Adaptation | Pollination | Reproduction | Dispersal

a) The production of offspring is called ....

b) An .... is something that makes an organism better suited to its environment.

c) .... is when something is spread out over an area.

d) The transfer of pollen to the stigma of a flower is called ....

3. **Tick a box next to each sentence to show whether it's an example of pollination or seed dispersal.**

	pollination	seed dispersal
A bee transferring pollen between flowers.	☐	☐
A conker dropping from a tree and rolling away.	☐	☐
A bird eating a cherry.	☐	☐
The wind blowing pollen grains out of cherry blossom.	☐	☐
A dog getting seeds stuck on its coat.	☐	☐
The wind blowing a dandelion 'clock'.	☐	☐

Pollination and Fertilisation

1. The diagram shows the structure of a flower.

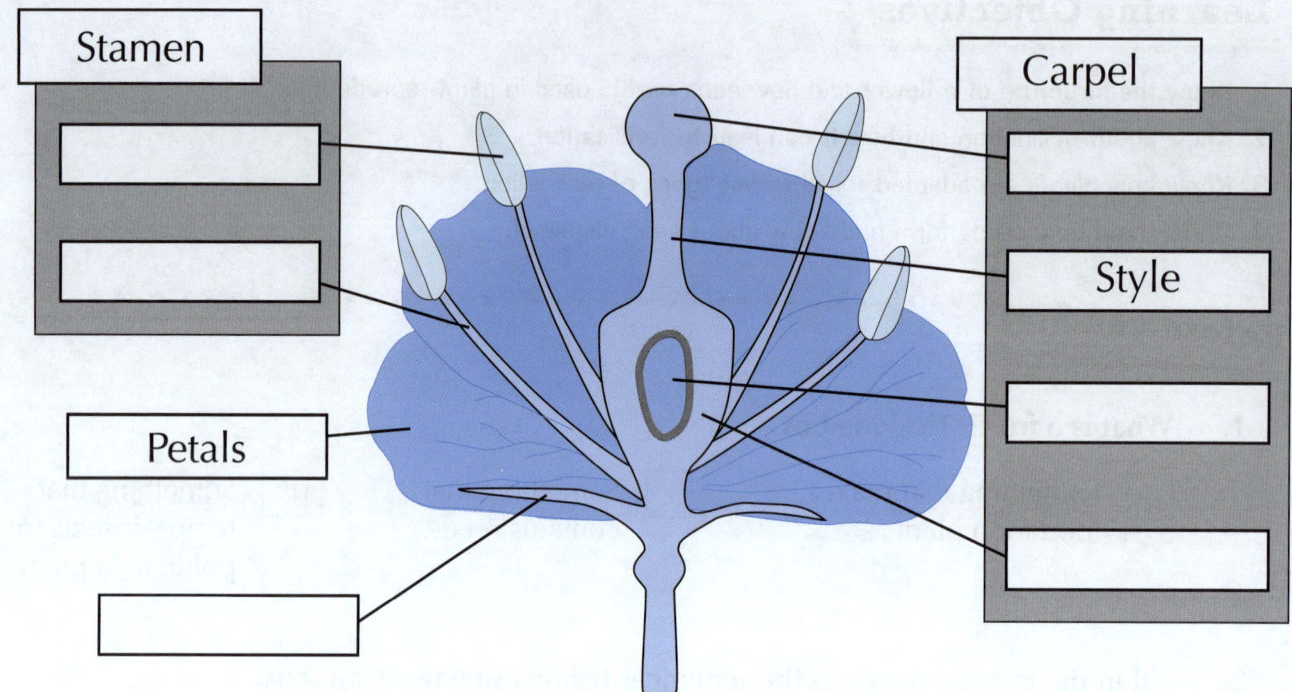

a) Label the diagram with the structures below.

Ovary Stigma Ovules

Filament Sepals Anther

b) What is the function of the style?

~~to look great~~ ....

c) Where are the female sex cells found?

....

d) Sepals are usually tougher than petals. Suggest why.

....

....

e) The stigmas of many plant species have sticky surfaces.
Why do you think this is useful for pollination?

....

....

Pollination and Fertilisation

2. Circle the correct words in the sentences below.

Pollen contains the **male / female** sex cells in plants. Pollen is found on the **anthers / filaments**. Pollen grains are transferred to the **petals / stigma** in the process of pollination. From there, the nucleus from the pollen travels to the **ovule / stamen**. This is where fertilisation takes place.

3. Are these statements true or false? Tick the correct boxes.

	True	False
a) Pollen can be transferred to another part of the same plant during pollination.	☐	☐
b) The joining of a nucleus from a male and female sex cell is called pollination.	☐	☐
c) A single plant can have flowers that produce both male and female sex cells.	☐	☐

4. Plants can either self-pollinate or cross-pollinate. Too much self-pollination can be a disadvantage to a plant and many plants are adapted to encourage some cross-pollination. In some plants, the anthers and stigmas on flowers start off far away from each other, but move closer together in flowers that have not been pollinated as they get older.

SCIENCE IN ACTION

a) What is the difference between self-pollination and cross-pollination?

....

....

....

b) What do you think is the benefit of the stigma and anthers being far apart in some plants?

....

....

....

c) Why do you think the stigma and anthers of older flowers that have not been pollinated move closer together in some plants?

....

....

Types of Pollination

1. Poppies are plants that are pollinated by insects.

a) Look at the photo of a poppy flower. Suggest how it is adapted for insect pollination.

Poppy flower

....

....

b) The photo shows a hazel tree flower.

Hazel tree flower

i) Sadiq says "The hazel tree flower isn't actually a flower because it doesn't have pretty petals". Do you agree? Why?

....

....

ii) How do you think a hazel tree is pollinated? Explain your answer.

....

....

iii) The pollen from plants like the hazel tree is often lighter than the pollen from plants like poppies. Why do you think this is?

....

....

2. Wheat is a wind-pollinated crop. Hena is a plant breeder who has grown a large number of wheat plants in a greenhouse. She is aiming to increase the grain size of her wheat by selecting the plants that produce the largest grains and breeding them together.

SCIENCE IN ACTION

a) While she is choosing which plants to breed together, Hena puts plastic bags around the flowers of each wheat plant in her greenhouse. Why do you think this is?

....

....

b) Hena selects two wheat plants with large grains. Using your knowledge about pollination, suggest a way to breed the two wheat plants together.

....

....

Seeds

1. In many plants, successful reproduction involves producing seeds.

a) What is a seed? Where does it develop from?

....

b) Label the diagram of a seed using the words below.

Seed coat

Embryo

Food store

c) What structure develops into a fruit around a seed?

....

2. Graham the cat has run through a hedge. Now he's covered in goose grass seeds.

goose grass seed

Graham

a) Explain how attaching to Graham's fur could help the goose grass seeds to grow better.

....

....

....

b) How are the seeds adapted to this method of seed dispersal?

....

c) Describe one other way that seeds can be dispersed by animals.

....

....

....

d) Some plants spread pollen when animals brush past their flowers and get pollen on their fur. How is this different from what's happened to Graham?

....

....

Seeds

3. Lucas wanted to investigate whether the distance sycamore seeds are dispersed is affected by the surface area of their wings. He made models of sycamore fruits using strips of paper for the wings and small balls of plasticine for the seeds. He made five models, each with different sized wings. He dropped each model three times from the same height above a fixed point on the ground. He measured the distance between the point above which the seed was dropped and where it landed. The results are shown in the table below.

PRACTICAL

Model	Surface area of each wing (cm^2)	Distance travelled (cm)			
		Drop 1	Drop 2	Drop 3	Average
1	1	4	5	6	5
2	2	16	19	10	15
3	3	20	27	22	
4	4	38	34	30	
5	5	27	28	26	

A sycamore fruit

MATHS SKILLS

a) Calculate the average distance travelled for each model.
The first two have been done already. Use your answers to complete the table.

b) Lucas talks to his friend Lee about his results.

Lucas: I thought models that had wings with bigger surface areas would travel further in my experiment, but model 5 doesn't fit this pattern.

Lee: Maybe that was because you didn't control the mass of the models.

Do you agree with Lee? Explain why.

How did you do?

Another topic done. Before dispersing away to the next one, check that you:

- [ ] Understand the functions in reproduction of the structures in a flower.
- [ ] Understand how plants are adapted for insect pollination or wind pollination.
- [ ] Understand what happens in pollination and fertilisation.
- [ ] Understand ways in which seeds are dispersed.

Topic 14 — Human Reproduction

It's time to learn about reproduction in humans. It's really rather different to how it happens in plants...

Learning Objectives

1. Know the structure of the human reproductive system and how each part is used in reproduction.
2. Understand the main stages of the menstrual cycle.
3. Know how a fertilised egg develops into a baby.
4. Understand how substances are transferred between the mother and the foetus, via the placenta.

Before you Start

1. **Which statement below is the correct function of the female reproductive system? Circle the correct answer.**

   To digest food and absorb nutrients.

   To create sex cells and protect the foetus.

   To move substances around the body.

   To fight against infections.

2. **Which of the statements about reproduction below are true and which are false? Tick the correct box.**

	True	False
Men produce sperm.	☐	☐
A lot of sperm fertilise each egg.	☐	☐
Women produce eggs.	☐	☐

3. **The diagrams below show an egg and some sperm. Which one shows the correct size of sperm compared to an egg? Tick the correct box.**

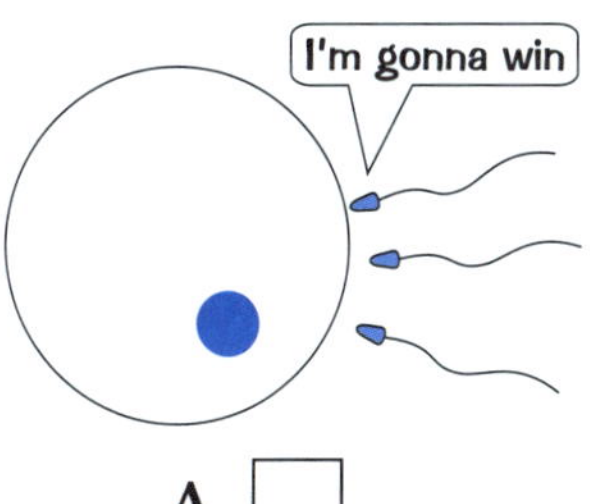

A ☐

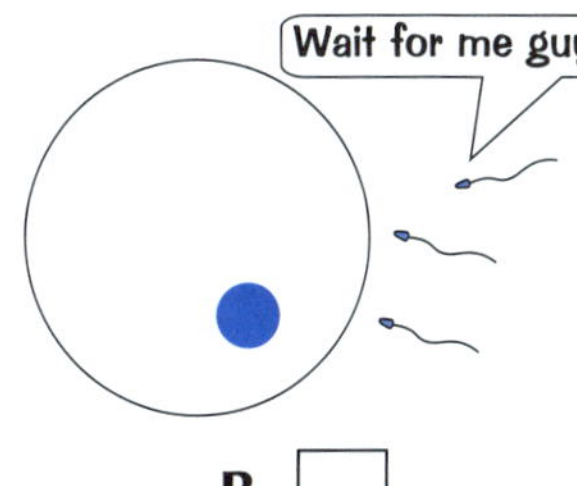

B ☐

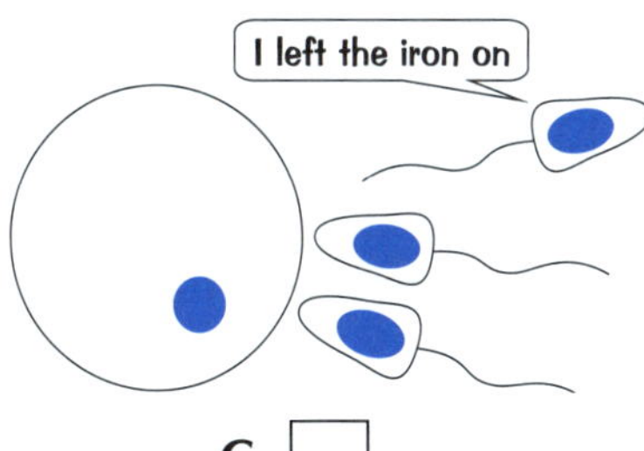

C ☐

4. **Which of the statements below is true? Tick the correct box.**

   ☐ A child only inherits characteristics from their mother.

   ☐ A child only inherits characteristics from their father.

   ☐ A child inherits characteristics from both their mother and their father.

Human Reproductive System

1. The sentences below are incorrect. For each one, give a correct version of the sentence.

a) Fertilisation happens inside the ovaries.

....

b) In a pregnant woman, the baby develops inside the tummy.

....

c) Sex cells are called embryos.

....

2. The diagram below shows the female reproductive system in humans.

a) Fill in the labels on the diagram using the words below. Not all the words are needed.

ovary	ovule	stigma	fallopian tube	vagina	uterus

b) Complete the sentences below by circling the correct word in each pair.

i) In the female reproductive system, eggs are stored in the **ovaries / uterus** .

ii) The release of an egg from this organ is called **gestation / ovulation** .

iii) When it's released, the egg moves into the **fallopian tube / ovule**

and travels towards the **uterus / ovary** .

c) Which part of the female reproductive system does sperm enter during sexual intercourse?

....

Human Reproductive System

3. The diagram below shows the male reproductive system in humans, with some parts of it labelled.

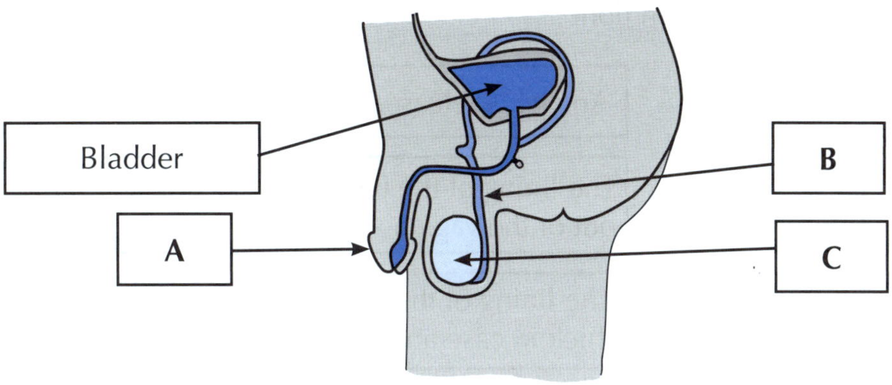

a) i) Name part **C**.

....

ii) What is the function of part **C**?

....

b) i) Name part **A**.

....

ii) Part **A** is covered by erectile tissue.
Describe what happens to erectile tissue during sexual intercourse.

....

iii) What happens to sperm at part **A** during sexual intercourse?

....

c) i) Part **B** is the vas deferens. It is a tube that carries sperm through the reproductive system. A vasectomy is an operation to cut the vas deferens, close to where it leaves part **C**. What happens to the transport of sperm from part **C** after a vasectomy.

....

ii) A vasectomy can be used to prevent pregnancy. Why do you think this is?

....

....

....

The Menstrual Cycle

1. The menstrual cycle has four main stages.

a) Draw lines to match each stage of the menstrual cycle with its correct description below. The first one has already been done.

Stage 1	An egg is released from one of the ovaries.
Stage 2	The lining of the uterus breaks down and passes out of the vagina — the woman has a period.
Stage 3	The lining of the uterus stays thick in case an egg is fertilised.
Stage 4	The lining of the uterus starts to build up.

b) How long does the average menstrual cycle last? ....

c) i) When in the menstrual cycle is the fertilisation of an egg most likely?

....

ii) Why is this the most likely time for fertilisation to happen?

....

....

iii) When in the menstrual cycle is the fertilisation of an egg least likely?

....

d i) What happens to the menstrual cycle if an egg is fertilised by a sperm?

....

ii) What does a fertilised egg develop into?

....

2. The contraceptive pill is a pill that women can take to prevent them from getting pregnant. The contraceptive pill works by stopping ovulation.

Why do you think this prevents pregnancy?

....

....

Fertilisation and Development

1. Fill in the blanks to complete the passage below.

Fertilisation occurs when the .... of a sperm and an egg join together.

Fertilisation of an egg normally happens in one of the ....

After fertilisation happens, the fertilised egg moves into the ....

It then .... in the wall of that organ.

The time between fertilisation and birth is called ....

2. The diagram below shows a timeline from the start to the end of pregnancy.

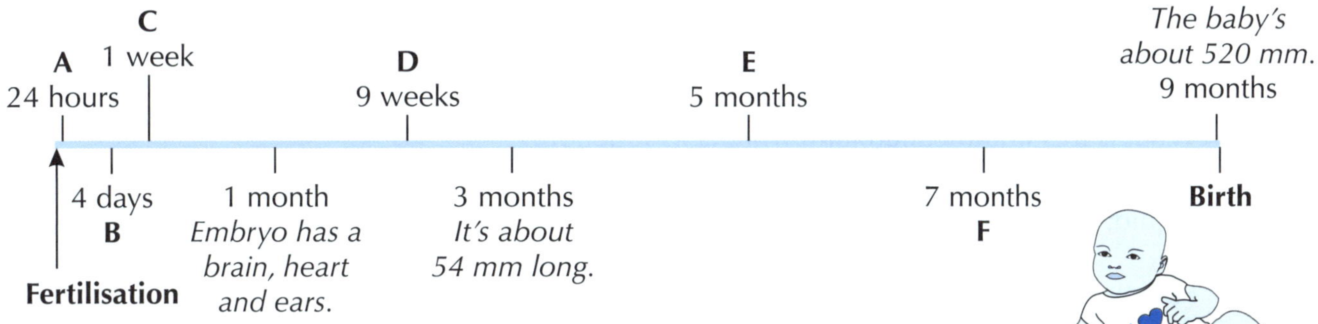

A 24 hours

C 1 week

D 9 weeks

E 5 months

The baby's about 520 mm. 9 months

Fertilisation

4 days **B**

1 month *Embryo has a brain, heart and ears.*

3 months *It's about 54 mm long.*

7 months **F**

Birth

I ♥ CGP

a) Write each letter from the timeline in the correct box below to match each of the events.

i) The baby would have a fair chance of surviving if born at this stage. ☐

ii) The embryo is around 25 mm long and is now called a foetus. ☐

iii) The fertilised egg cell divides into two. ☐

iv) Implantation into the wall of the uterus happens. ☐

v) The foetus is around 160 mm long and it kicks. ☐

vi) The fertilised egg has divided into 32 cells and is now called an embryo. ☐

b) Explain what happens to these parts of the female reproductive system during birth.

i) The muscular wall of the uterus

....

ii) The cervix and vagina

....

Fertilisation and Development

3. The placenta is an organ that lets substances move between the mother and developing foetus.

The table below shows whether substances are transferred from the mother to the foetus, or from the foetus to the mother via the placenta.

Mother to foetus	Foetus to mother
oxygen	

a) Write the following substances in the correct columns of the table.

carbon dioxide nutrients waste products

b) What connects the placenta to the foetus? ....

c) The foetus is surrounded by a liquid inside the uterus.
What is this liquid called, and what is its function?

Liquid: ....

Function: ....

d) Why do you think oxygen and carbon dioxide move in and out of the baby through the placenta, instead of the baby's lungs?

....

....

4. Infertility is when people struggle to get pregnant and have a baby.

a) Some women with fertility problems have blocked fallopian tubes.
Why do you think this could make it hard for a woman to get pregnant?

....

....

b) Some men with fertility problems have sperm that can't swim properly.
Why do you think this could cause a man to be infertile?

....

....

Fertilisation and Development

5. Read these passages from a leaflet about the effect of caffeine during pregnancy, and answer the questions that follow.

Caffeine is found in some food and drink, such as coffee, tea and chocolate. It can cause the heart rate and blood pressure to increase.

Caffeine can cross the placenta into the blood of a foetus. Having more than 200 mg of caffeine per day can increase the risk of premature birth and low birth weight. It also increases the risk of miscarriage.

	Caffeine content
Cup of coffee	100 mg
Cup of tea	75 mg
Can of cola	40 mg
Can (250 ml) of energy drink	up to 80 mg
50 g bar of plain chocolate	up to 25 mg

a) What do you think is meant by 'premature birth'?

....

b) i) Using the information above, work out how much caffeine per day the pregnant women described below could be having.

MATHS SKILLS

Irene drinks 2 cups of tea a day. ....

Alex drinks 1 cup of coffee and 2 cans of energy drink a day. ....

ii) Which of the two women drinks too much caffeine per day?

....

c) A scientist wants to test how caffeine affects pregnancy. He tests it by giving different amounts of caffeine to mice. Why does the scientist test the effect of caffeine on pregnancy in mice rather than humans?

....

....

How did you do?

I don't know about you, but I think going from a tiny egg to a crying, eating, pooping baby in 9 months is just a little bit impressive. And hopefully you now:

- ☐ Know the structure of the human reproductive system.
- ☐ Understand the menstrual cycle.
- ☐ Know how a fertilised egg develops.
- ☐ Understand how substances are transferred to a baby via the placenta.

Topic 15 — Evolution

Time for an exciting look at natural selection, evolution and biodiversity. Hold on to your hats...

Learning Objectives

1. Understand the process of natural selection and how variation leads to it.
2. Understand why some species go extinct.
3. Understand the theory of evolution.
4. Know why biodiversity is important.
5. Know how gene banks can be used to preserve biodiversity.

Before you Start

1. Tick whether the features below are inherited, environmental or a mixture of both.

	inherited	environmental	both
Having green eyes	☐	☐	☐
Having a scar from an operation	☐	☐	☐
Having big muscles	☐	☐	☐

2. Which of the sentences below are true? Tick the correct boxes.

A The species alive today are the same as the ones alive two million years ago. ☐

B Organisms have changed to adapt to their environments. ☐

C All individuals within a species are exactly the same. ☐

D A fossil is the preserved remains or traces of an organism. ☐

3. The species in the box below are all found in meadows near a farm. Use the words to answer the questions below.

grass hawk blackbird caterpillar rabbit

a) In the box on the right, draw a food web for the species in the list.

b) Which one species is a producer?

....

c) Which two species are predators?

....

d) Which two species compete for food? ....

Natural Selection

1. Use the words from the box to complete the sentences about natural selection. You do not need to use all the words.

parents	variation	genes	offspring	competing
reproduce	cheese	extinct	eat	adapted

In a group of organisms, there can be .... in characteristics.

Some individuals have more useful characteristics, which will help them to be

better at .... This means that they're more likely to survive

and ....

Parents can then pass these useful characteristics on to their ....

The characteristics are passed on in their ....

Over several generations, the population becomes .... to its

environment — this is natural selection. If no individuals in the population have useful

characteristics for their environment, the species could go ....

2. The hummingbirds shown below eat nectar from flowers. The flowers are very long, with the nectar at the bottom. There is competition between hummingbirds for the nectar.

a) What is meant by competition?

....

....

b) i) What characteristic of the hummingbirds above shows variation?

....

ii) How do you think this characteristic will help the hummingbirds compete for food?

Hummm

....

....

....

Natural Selection

3. Read the scientific report below and answer the questions that follow.

Mining can have devastating effects on the environment. The soil around mines can be contaminated with metals like mercury and nickel. These metals are poisonous to many plants. They can stop seeds from sprouting, make plants struggle to grow or even kill the plants.

Horston mine opened in 1990 and contaminated nearby soil. We investigated a plant species growing on soil contaminated by Horston mine. Some plants were able to survive in the contaminated soil and some couldn't. Every five years we measured the percentage of individual plants in this species that survived to the following year. The results are shown in the table above.

Year	Percentage of plants that survived
1990	5
1995	10
2000	20
2005	35
2010	40
2015	45

a) Plot the data from the table above in the graph on the right. Plot the points as crosses and join them with lines.

Don't forget to label your axes.

b) Describe the results shown in your graph.

....

....

....

....

....

c) What do you think the scientists would find if they investigated the plants in 2020?

....

d) Why do you think this data shows evidence for natural selection?

Hint: being able to survive in contaminated soil is a useful characteristic for a plant.

....

....

....

e) A rare plant was only found in the area near Horston mine.
Seeds of this species could never sprout if there was a lot of metal in the soil.
What do you think happened to this species after the mine opened? Explain your answer.

....

....

Theory of Evolution

1. Charles Darwin published his theory of evolution in 1859.

a) What is evolution?

....

....

b) How does natural selection cause evolution to happen?

....

....

c) An online article said, "Evolution has a purpose, and its purpose is to make a perfect organism". Do you agree? Why?

....

....

2. Read the following passage and answer the questions below.

Chelonians are a group of reptiles that include turtles, tortoises and terrapins. These species have hard shells made up of bony plates.

Fossils of the earliest known turtle, *E. africanus*, have been found in South Africa. This species lived around 260 million years ago. Its ribs had evolved to be wider and flatter than in other reptiles. It didn't have a shell.

a) Based on the information about *E. africanus*, suggest how the shell of a turtle evolved.

....

....

....

b) How do you think Chelonians evolved to have shells?

....

....

....

....

Biodiversity

1. Costa Rica is a country in Central America. It has a large area of rainforest. Pabla, Paulo and Juan talk about their experience of the rainforest below.

Pabla: I'm a tour guide. Most tourists want to go into the rainforest because of its high biodiversity. They want to see all the birds, butterflies and other animals. Some tourists really want to see the great green macaw, but its population has decreased due to trees being cut down.

Paulo: I live in the rainforest with my family. We eat many different plants and animals from the forest. I am also a Shaman and so have been taught how to use the plants that grow here to heal people's diseases.

Juan: I work in a seed bank, which is a type of gene bank. We collect seeds from trees and store them. The seeds may be used to replant forests and increase biodiversity. This helps to prevent populations of other organisms from getting too small. Preventing populations from getting too small means there's likely to be more variation between organisms.

Use the information above to help you answer the questions below.

a) i) What does Pabla mean when she says the rainforest has 'high biodiversity'?

....

....

ii) What does Pabla mean by the term 'population'?

....

b) Give one resource that humans may struggle to get if rainforest biodiversity decreases.

....

c) i) Juan works in a gene bank. What is the purpose of a gene bank?

....

ii) Why do you think replanting forests helps to prevent populations of other organisms from getting too small?

....

....

iii) Preventing populations in the rainforest from getting too small helps to protect them from extinction if their environment changes. Why do you think this is?

Think back to your work on natural selection to help with this question.

....

....

....

Biodiversity

2. Some scientists ran a biodiversity experiment over 10 years. They removed starfish from a shore line and counted the number of other species that were there each year. The graph below shows their results.

a) i) How many species were present three years after the starfish were removed?

....

ii) Calculate the percentage change in number of species from when starfish were removed to 10 years after the experiment started. Give your answer to one decimal place.

MATHS SKILLS

.....................%

Starfish removed

Number of species present

Time (Years)

The starfish were predators of mussels. Mussels have hard shells and live on rocks. The mussels compete with other species in the ecosystem for space and food.

b) i) What do you think happened to the number of mussels after starfish were removed?

....

ii) Explain the effect this could have on the rest of the populations of species in the ecosystem.

....

....

....

c) The scientists are planning to do the starfish removal experiment again on some other shore lines. Why do you think the scientists want to do this?

....

....

How did you do?

Well, that's it for evolution and biodiversity. Fascinating stuff really. Hopefully by now you:

- ☐ Understand natural selection.
- ☐ Know why some species go extinct.
- ☐ Understand the theory of evolution.
- ☐ Know why biodiversity is important.
- ☐ Know how gene banks can be used to preserve biodiversity.

Mixed Questions

Now you've got through all that, it's time for some mixed practice.
Have a go at these without looking at your notes, to see what you know, and what you don't.

1. Bim and Jay use chromatography to investigate the different dyes that make up a food dye used to colour sweets.

a) Why was chromatography an appropriate separation technique for Bim and Jay to use?

....

1 mark

The diagram below shows their apparatus. The food dye is dye number 6.

Beaker
Paper
Water
dye spots
base line
1 2 3 4 5 6 dye number

b) Write down the name of the solvent used by Bim and Jay.

....

1 mark

c) Which dye was not soluble in the solvent?

....

1 mark

d) Which of dyes 1-5 were definitely not in the sweets?

....

1 mark

2. When unbalanced forces act on an object they can have a number of effects, including making the object move faster or slower.

a) Write down **two** more possible effects of unbalanced forces acting on an object.

1. ....

2. ....

2 marks

b) The forces on a car are balanced. Only two of the statements below about the car could possibly be true. Tick the **two** statements that could be true.

☐ it's stationary ☐ it's slowing down

☐ it's accelerating ☐ it's travelling at a constant speed

☐ it's turning a corner

2 marks

Mixed Questions

c) Dev is standing still. He says "the forces on me must be balanced because I'm not moving, but the only force I can think of is the force of gravity pulling me down". Explain to Dev why the forces are actually balanced.

....

....

....

2 marks

3. The diagram shows a circuit containing a cell, an ammeter and one bulb.

Circuit 1:

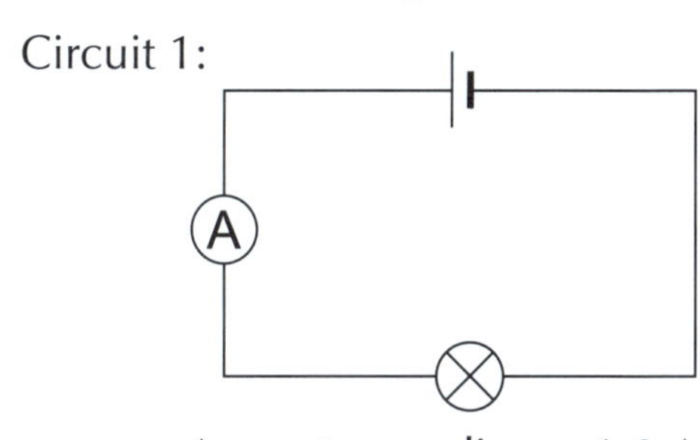

Ammeter reading = 1.0 A

a) Write down the ammeter readings for circuit 2 and circuit 3 below. All cells and bulbs are identical.

i) Circuit 2:

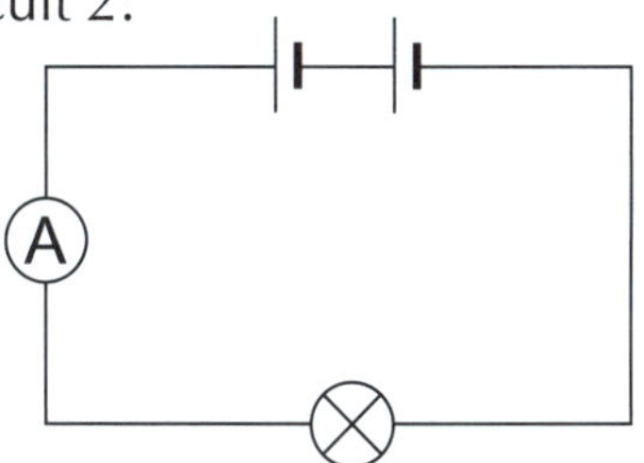

Ammeter reading = ... A

ii) Circuit 3:

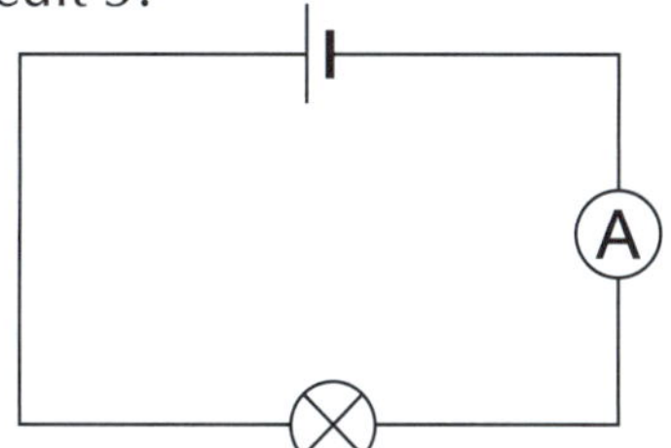

Ammeter reading = ... A

2 marks

b) Look at the circuit below and complete the table to show the current readings on the ammeters.

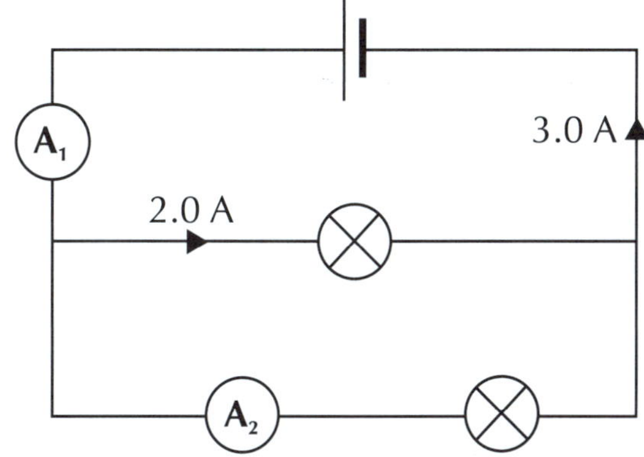

Ammeter	Current (A)
A_1	
A_2	

2 marks

Mixed Questions

4. Below is a diagram of the menstrual cycle.

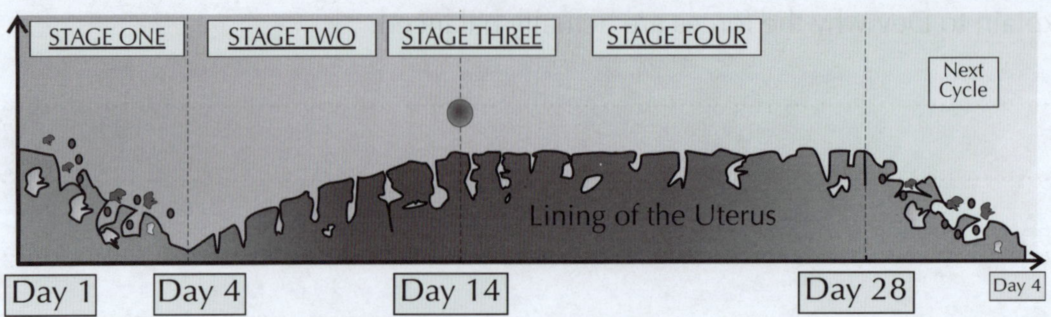

a) Danni is trying to get pregnant. However, her body has a lower level of a substance called Hormone A, which causes the uterus lining to thicken.

i) Which stage of the diagram does Hormone A affect?

....

1 mark

ii) Explain why having a low level of Hormone A might make it harder for Danni to get pregnant.

....

....

....

2 marks

b) After some time, Danni does becomes pregnant. When she becomes pregnant, Stage One of the menstrual cycle doesn't happen and the cycle doesn't continue.

i) Name the process that is happening at Stage One of the menstrual cycle.

....

1 mark

ii) Explain why Stage One is stopped when Danni becomes pregnant.

....

....

2 marks

c) During her pregnancy, the doctors advise Danni to stop drinking alcohol because it could harm the foetus. Explain how alcohol would be able to harm the foetus if Danni drinks it.

....

....

1 mark

Mixed Questions

5. Carly is balancing a ball on her outstretched leg.
The diagram below shows the muscles involved in the movement.

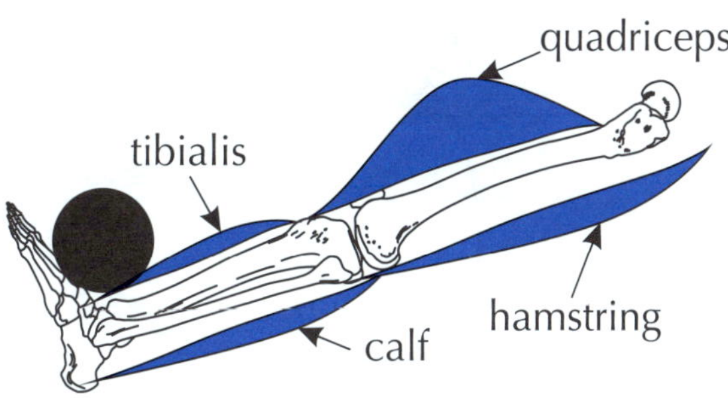

a) The quadriceps is part of a pair of muscles that work against each other to cause movement.
Name the muscle that works against the quadriceps.

....

1 mark

b) i) What will happen to the ball Carly is balancing if her quadriceps relaxes?
Explain why this will happen.

....

....

....

3 marks

ii) What will happen to the ball Carly is balancing if her calf contracts?

....

1 mark

6. When an acid and an alkali are added together, a salt is formed.

a) Which acid and alkali react to produce potassium sulfate? Tick **one** box.

sodium hydroxide and sulfuric acid ☐

potassium hydroxide and nitric acid ☐

sodium hydroxide and nitric acid ☐

potassium hydroxide and sulfuric acid ☐

1 mark

b) Acids can also be reacted with metals. What **two** products would be produced if magnesium was reacted with hydrochloric acid?

1. ....

2. ....

2 marks

Mixed Questions

7. The diagram below shows what happens when sunlight shines onto a raindrop.

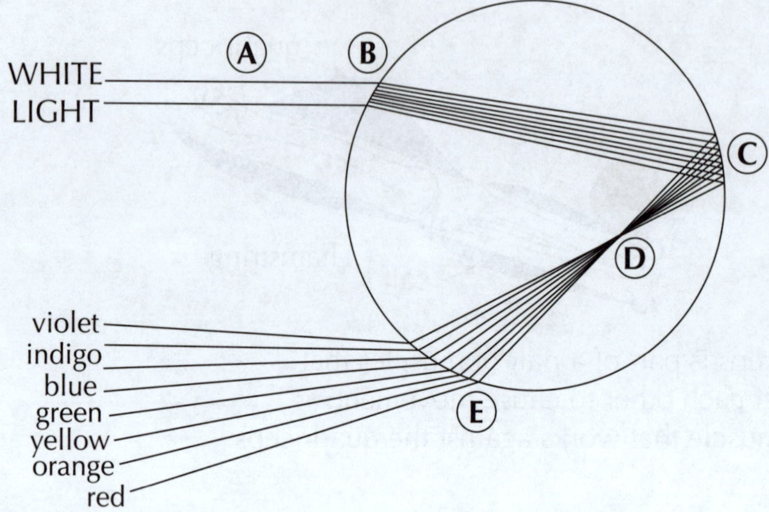

a) Write a letter that corresponds to a place on the diagram where each of the following effects is occurring.

Refraction: ....   Reflection: ....

2 marks

b) What happens to the ray of white light as it enters the raindrop? Tick **two** correct answers.

- ☐ it speeds up
- ☐ it continues along a straight line
- ☐ it bends towards the normal
- ☐ it slows down
- ☐ it continues with the same speed
- ☐ it bends away from the normal

2 marks

c) Why is coloured light leaving the raindrop at point **E** when white light entered the raindrop at point **B**?

....

....

2 marks

d) What colour light would be seen if there was a blue filter at point **E**? Explain why.

....

....

....

2 marks

You'll have completed this book in 5, 4, 3, 2 ....

That's it, you've finished! Time for a nice cuppa / marshmallow / sit down (delete as appropriate)... Oh and to mark this lot of course. If you didn't score very highly, have a look back at the answers for the questions you struggled with to see what you should have written. Then you'll know for next time.

Score: ☐ / **37**

Answers

Topic 1 — Distance-Time Graphs

Page 2 — Before you Start

1 Speed tells you how much **distance** is travelled in how much **time**.

2 a car travelling at 55 km/h

3 a) Distance = speed × time = 30 × 2 = **60 km**

b) Distance = speed × time = 8 × 10 = **80 m**

4 a) Rohan b) Austin

Pages 3-4 — Using Distance-Time Graphs

1 a) 3 s b) 10 m c) 9 s

2 a) 60 km b) 1.5 hours c) 0.5 hours

d) i) 40 km ii) 30 minutes

3 a) A straight line.

b) A curved line getting steeper.

4 a) Speed = distance ÷ time = 30 ÷ 15 = **2 m/s**

b) i) It's slowing down.

ii) It's speeding up.

c) It's not moving.

d) The line would be straight and rising at the beginning. It will later curve until it has levelled off.

Page 5 — Drawing Distance-Time Graphs

1 a)

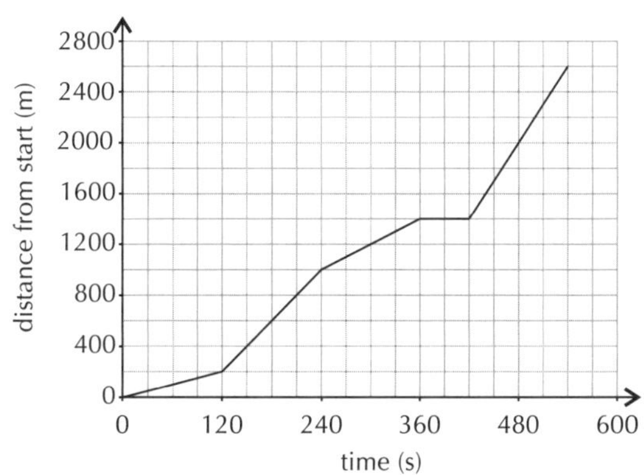

b) E.g. it would provide more information about how Radha's speed changes over time, so it would be easier to tell when Radha is accelerating and when she is moving at a constant speed.

Topic 2 — Forces

Page 6 — Before you Start

1 True

False

2 slow down, drag, opposite to

3 ice

Ice is slippy so produces less friction than dry pavement.

4

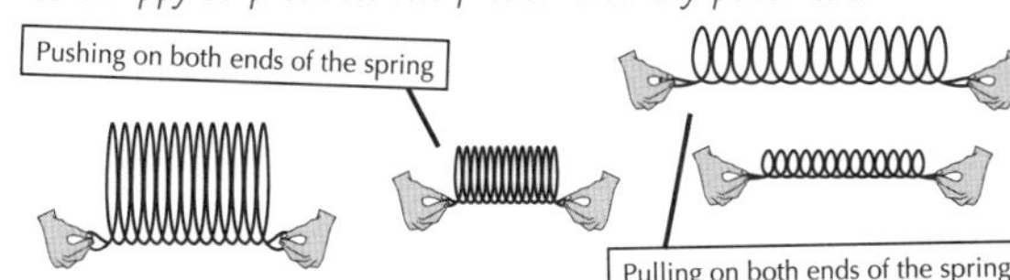

Page 7 — Types of Force

1 a) Air resistance.

b) The tension in the stretched elastic band.

c) Friction and air resistance.

2 newtons

3 a) A force that acts between two objects that aren't touching.

b) E.g. friction / a supporting force from the table

4 E.g. the student could pull the box with a string attached to a newton meter. This would display the force the student is using to pull the box as they pull it.

Pages 8-10 — Balanced and Unbalanced Forces

1 Diagrams B and D should be circled.

For forces to be balanced, they have to be the same size AND acting in exactly opposite directions.

2 a) E.g.

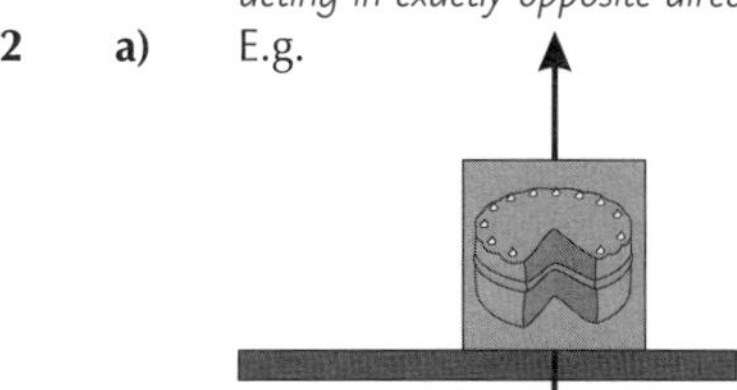

The box isn't moving but gravity is still pulling the box down and the shelf is producing an equal and opposite force that is pushing the box up.

b) E.g. Saskia is right. Because the box was falling down, a force acting upwards was needed to stop the box from falling. This must have been created by Saskia's arms.

3 2.5 – 1.0 = **1.5 N**

4 a) 0 N

For the bike to be travelling in a straight line at a constant speed, there must be no resultant force acting on the bike. Any resultant force would cause a change in its speed or direction.

b) The path of the bike will curve in the direction of the force due to the gust of wind.

5 a) i) cannot tell

ii) The forces are the same size, which means that they're balanced. When forces are balanced this means that an object can't be changing speed or direction. It can either be stationary or moving at a constant speed.

b) A. It has the biggest difference between the up and down forces, and the biggest difference between the right and left forces.

6 a) Neither. Leigh is wrong because an object can be moving if the forces acting on it are in equilibrium. It will move at a constant speed. Petra is wrong because even though there is a forward force, there is an equal force acting in the opposite direction, so it can't be speeding up.

b) Resultant force = forward force – backward force

Forward force = 500 + 250 = 750 N

Backward force = 500 – 100 = 400 N

Resultant force = 750 – 400 = **350 N (in the forward direction)**

Pages 11-12— Friction and Resistance

1 a)

3 rough surface 1 smooth surface 2

Even though they're both on smooth surfaces, number 1 is faster than number 2, because number 1 has a more streamlined shape so will be slowed down less by air resistance.

b) contact force

A contact force is a force that acts between two objects that are touching.

c) The object will move down the slope more quickly than it did outside the vacuum box. This is because there is no air resistance in the vacuum box, so only the friction from the slope will oppose the object's movement.

2 a) E.g. snow is slippery so there is low friction between the snow and the wheels. This means that the tyres/wheels can't grip the snow and so they just spin.

b) E.g. the rough board is rougher than the snow so this creates more friction between the tyres and the ground. This means that the van will be able to move more easily on the board than on the snow.

Answers

3 **a)** The rocket has a streamlined shape / it is thin at the top and slowly gets wider further down. This means that it is easier for the rocket to cut/slip through the air, which will reduce the air resistance that acts on the rocket.

b) The downward force of gravity/weight doesn't change when the parachute opens. The upward force of air resistance increases a lot when the parachute opens.

Pages 13-14 — Forces and Elasticity

1 Brooklyn. The force is only acting at one end of the spring. This means that it will move in the direction of that force. For it to change shape / compress / stretch, a force would need to be acting at both ends of the spring.

2 **when the wheel moves over the speed bump**: The length of the spring will decrease because it will be compressed due to the upward force of the speed bump and the downward force of the weight of the car.
when the car is raised above the ground: The length of the spring will increase because it will stretch due to the downward force of the weight of the wheel and the upwards reaction force of the car jack lifting the car.

3 **a)** Energy is transferred from Rochelle's kinetic energy store to the rope's elastic potential energy store.

b) The rope is elastic so it will spring back to its original shape. When this happens, energy is transferred from the rope's elastic potential energy store to Rochelle's kinetic energy store, causing her to bounce back up into the air.

4 If the material obeyed Hooke's law, then the graph would show that the amount the material extends is directly proportional to the force / the relationship would be linear / the graph would be a straight line. The graph shows a curved line, which means that the material doesn't obey Hooke's law.

Topic 3 — Gravity

Page 15 — Before you Start

1 False, True, False, False

2 the paper clip
The air resistance acting on the bank note will be much larger, so it is likely to fall more slowly than the paper clip.

3 the Earth, the Sun, the Moon
All objects exert a gravitational force.

Pages 16-19 — Gravity

1 **a)** A gravitational field is the area around an object where other objects feel a gravitational force.

b) D
The force due to the Earth's gravitational field is downwards towards the surface of the Earth. An arrow showing this force should start from the object and point directly downwards towards the Earth.

2 **a)** Mass is the amount of stuff in an object (measured in kg), while weight is the force of gravity on an object that has mass (measured in newtons).
The mass of an object doesn't change but weight changes if the gravitational field strength changes.

b) The force from gravity on a 1 kg mass.

3 **a) i)** weight = mass × gravitational field strength/g

ii) Dice B has the greater weight, because it has the greater mass, and the force due to gravity increases with mass.

b) E.g. I disagree with Austin. Every object that falls only due to the force of gravity will fall at the same rate, so dice A and B should hit the floor at the same time.
You don't need to worry about the effect of air resistance here because both dice are the same shape and they're only dropped from a small height above the ground.

c) E.g.

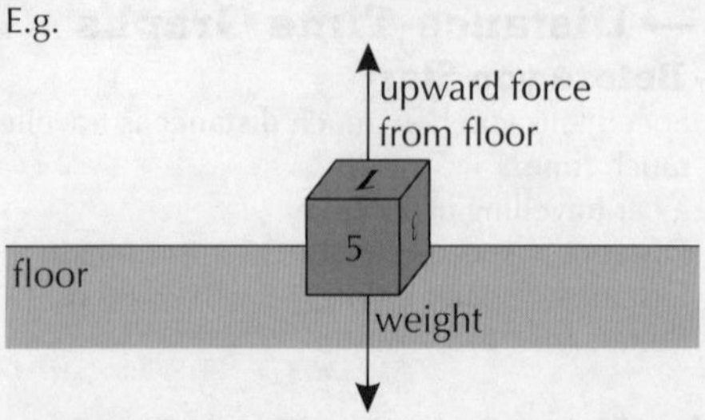

upward force
from floor
floor
weight

d) Similarity: e.g. they are both non-contact forces / they're both caused by fields
Difference: e.g. magnetic forces only act between magnetic materials but gravitational forces act between all objects (with mass) / magnetic forces can be attractive or repulsive but gravitational forces are always attractive.

4 **a) i)** 10 N/kg

ii) weight = mass × gravitational field strength
Rearrange the equation for mass:
mass = weight ÷ gravitational field strength
= 800 ÷ 10 = **80 kg**

b) It causes the Moon to change direction.
It's the pull of the Earth's gravity that makes the Moon move in a (rough) circle instead of travelling straight on.

c) i) 80 kg
The mass of an object is a property of that object — no matter where they are, their mass will be the same. So your answer should be the same as your answer to part a)ii).

ii) weight = mass × gravitational field strength
= 80 × 1.6 = **128 N**

d) The force due to gravity on the rocket from the Moon will decrease as the rocket moves away from the Moon. The further the rocket gets from the Moon, the less force the engine needs to apply to balance the Moon's gravity.

5 **a)** E.g. the greater the height, the lower the weight.

b) The weight of the ball decreases as the height above the base of the mountain increases because weight is the force due to gravity, and the force due to gravity decreases as the distance from the centre of Earth increases.

c) E.g. the graph would show a similar slope / slope down in the same way, but the values of weight would be twice those in the graph. This is because weight is proportional to the mass of the object and the gravitational field strength, and the mass has been doubled while the gravitational field strength remains the same.

Topic 4 — Circuits

Page 20 — Before you Start

1 0
The switch is open so there's a gap in the circuit. The circuit must be complete for any of the bulbs to light up.

2 Both bulbs will go out.
This is because the broken bulb causes a gap in the circuit.

3 **a)** E.g. the water is not used up / there is a continuous flow all the way round / the water is driven around the circuit (by the pump).

b) E.g. the water pipes are hollow and wires are not. / water leaks out if a pipe breaks but current doesn't leak out of a broken wire.

Pages 21-22 — Resistance

1 Resistance = Potential Difference ÷ Current

2 **a)** Material 2

b) Material 1

c) 6 V
The potential difference across the test material could never be greater than the potential difference of the battery.

Answers

3 a) E.g.

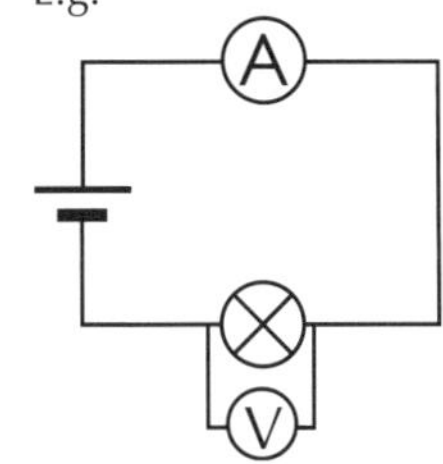

The voltmeter should be parallel to the bulb, and there shouldn't be any other components.

b) Resistance = Potential Difference ÷ Current:
1 ÷ 0.25 = **4 Ω**
2 ÷ 0.40 = **5 Ω**
3 ÷ 0.50 = **6 Ω**

Potential difference (V)	Current (A)	Resistance (Ω)
1	0.25	**4**
2	0.40	**5**
3	0.50	**6**
4	0.58	6.9

c) The bulb may break if its potential difference rating is lower than the potential difference rating of the cell.

d) E.g. a large current can cause the wires or components in the circuit to heat up, which is dangerous because it can cause fires/burns.

Pages 23-24 — Series Circuits

1 True, False, False, True

2 a) i) Paula is wrong. In a series circuit the current is not shared between components, so the current through the bulbs will be the same as the reading on A_1.

ii) Kai is wrong. Current does not get used up. In a series circuit the current is always the same, so the readings on A_1 and A_2 will be the same.

b) i) The readings on A_1 and A_2 will decrease.
The current in the circuit will be smaller because adding the extra bulb increases the resistance.

ii) Kai is correct. In a series circuit the potential difference is shared across the components.
So adding a third bulb means the potential difference across each bulb is smaller and each bulb is dimmer.

3 a) 3 V
In a series circuit the potential difference of the power source is shared across the components. Since resistor 1 has a 7 V share, resistor 2 must have a 3 V share.

b) Resistor 1. Resistance is equal to the potential difference divided by the current. The circuit is a series circuit, so the current through both resistors will be the same. Resistor 1 has a higher potential difference so its resistance must also be higher.

Pages 25-26 — Parallel Circuits

1 a) None of the motors will run.
b) Motor 1 and Motor 2
c) Motor 1 and Motor 3
d) It has components/motors on separate loops.

2 a) $A_5 = 12 - (5 + 1 + 2) = 12 - 8 = \mathbf{4\ A}$
The currents in the branches add together to make the total current. The total current is 12 A, so A_5 must be 4 A.
$A_6 = \mathbf{12\ A}$
The current combines before A_6, so the current at A_6 is the same as at A_1.

b) He should put one switch on each separate loop, either before or after the bulb.

c) E.g. if one bulb breaks, the other bulbs will still work. / The bulbs will be brighter because the potential difference across them will be greater.

3 a) Circuit B. Circuit B is a parallel circuit, so the potential difference across each loop is the same as the potential difference of the cell, 6 V. Circuit A is a series circuit, so the total potential difference is divided between all the components, meaning the potential difference across each bulb is 3 V.

b) Erin is correct. The potential difference across the bulbs won't change so they will be the same brightness.

c) The bulbs will be brighter because more energy will be transferred from the moving charge to the bulbs.

Topic 5 — Light and Vision

Page 27 — Before you Start

1 Water

2

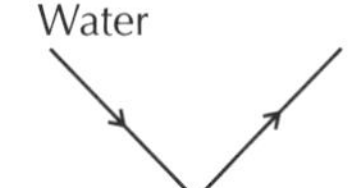

Remember, light travels in straight lines and reflects at the same angle at which it hits the surface.

3 absorbed, transmitted, translucent, transparent, reflected, reflected.

Pages 28-29 — Refraction

1 a) A medium is a substance that light travels through.
b) glass
c) towards
d) i)

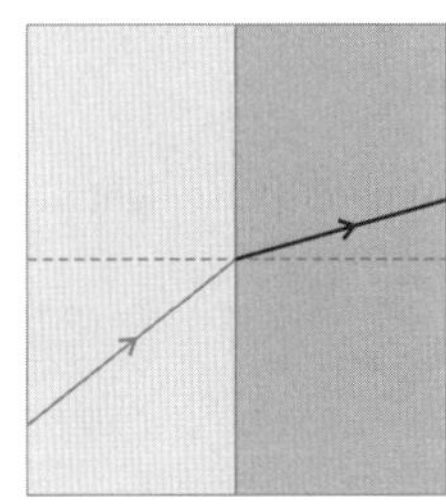

ii)

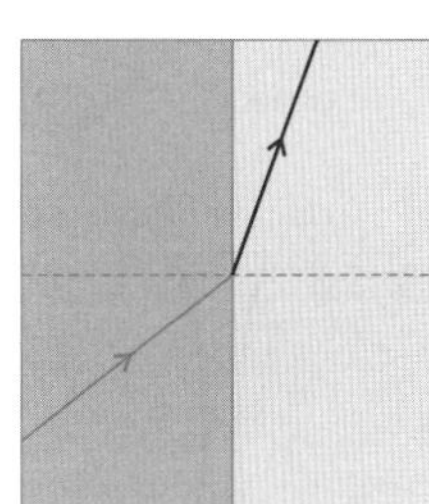

You don't have to get the angles exactly the same as here — what's important is which way the ray bends compared to the normal. This is the same for part e.

iii)

e)

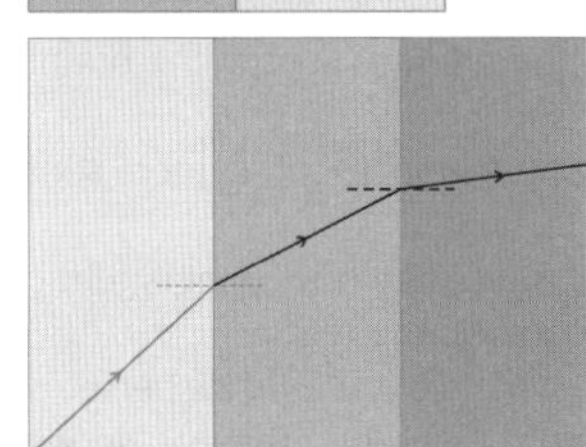

2 a)

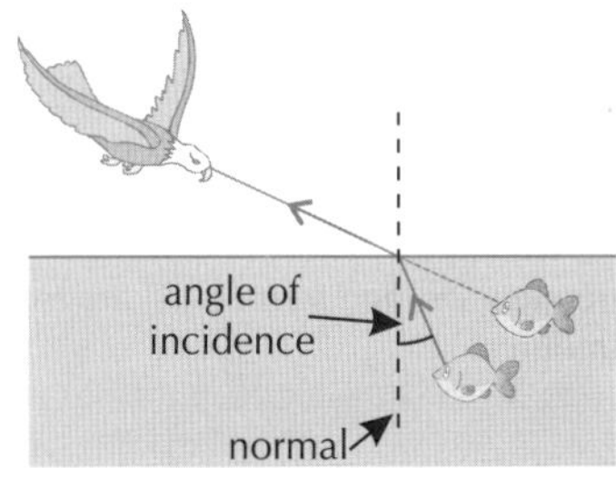

Answers

b) The light bends away from the normal as it moves from water to air, so water must be more dense.
c) It would be closer.
d)

Pages 30-32 — Vision

1 a)

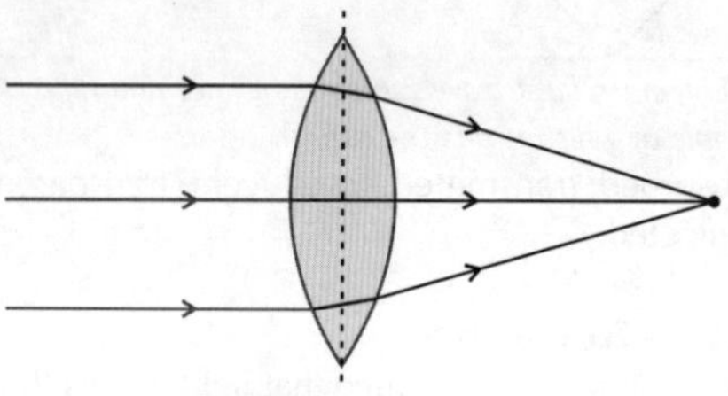

b)

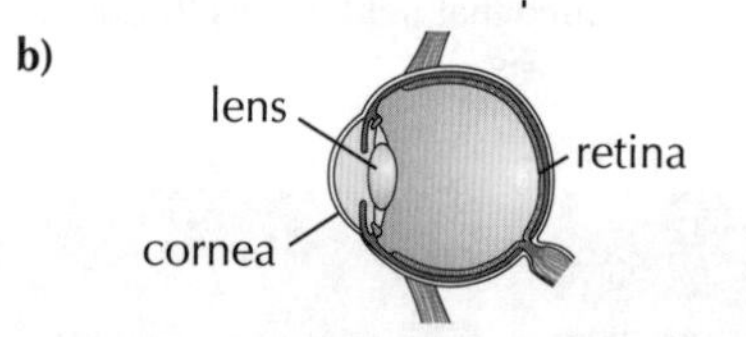

c) Concave lenses spread out / disperse light.
d) E.g.

2 a) Convex.
b)

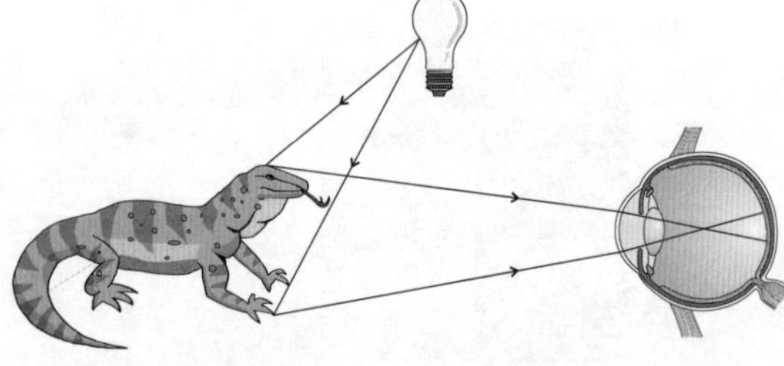

c) The signal from the retina is sent to the brain.

3 a) E.g. a lamp, the sun.
b) retina, photosensitive, electrical, camera sensor.

4 a) The eyeball is too long.
b) E.g. Because it can change how light is refracted to make sure light is focused on the retina.
c) A concave lens, because it would disperse / spread out the light rays before they enter the eye, so it will be further until they are brought together at a focus.

Pages 33-34 — Colour

1 a) The light would be split into colours / have a rainbow / spectrum effect.
b) frequencies, white
c) Different frequencies, and so colours, are refracted by different amounts.

2 a)

Event	Colour that object appears	Colour(s) absorbed
White light hits a white object	White	None
Green light hits a white object	Green	None
White light hits a blue object	Blue	All except blue
Red light hits a blue object	Black	All/Red

b) E.g. The room may not be dark enough, meaning that light entering the room from another source could be reflected by the object.

3 a) A filter does not change the frequency of light. A red filter absorbs all the colours of light except for red light, which it lets through.
b) Magenta
c) The clown
d) Have all three colours of light shining at the stage — together they will produce white light.

Topic 6 — Wave Effects

Page 35 — Before you Start

1 Amplitude — The displacement from the rest position to the crest of the wave.
Frequency — The number of waves per second.
Wavelength — The distance between two peaks of a wave.

2 A longitudinal wave with vibrations in the direction of wave travel.

3

Sound cannot travel through...	Sound can travel through...		
A vacuum	Air	Wood	Water

4

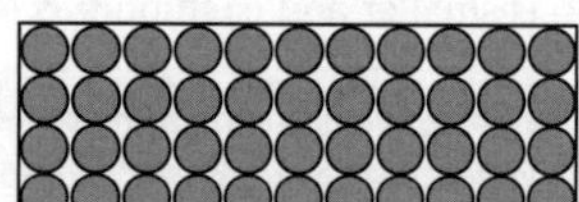

Pages 36-37 — Waves and Energy

1 a) i) True ii) True iii) False
b) i) high pitched and loud
ii) The energy transferred by a wave increases with its frequency and amplitude. A higher pitch means a higher frequency and a louder sound means a higher amplitude.

2 a) E.g. ultraviolet light cannot be seen by the human eye, whereas visible light can be. Ultraviolet light has a higher frequency than visible light.
b) Visible light has a lower frequency than ultraviolet light, which means it has less energy.
c) X-rays are likely to be damaging to living cells since they have a higher frequency then ultraviolet, which means they transfer more energy.

3 a) up and down, energy, pressure wave, energy
b) It will increase the power of the waves. An increased height means an increased amplitude, which will lead to more energy being transferred over the same time.
c) Location C — it has the highest average wind speed. This means it would, on average have the biggest waves and so the waves would transfer the most energy over time.

Answers

Pages 38-39 — Pressure Waves

1 a) E.g.

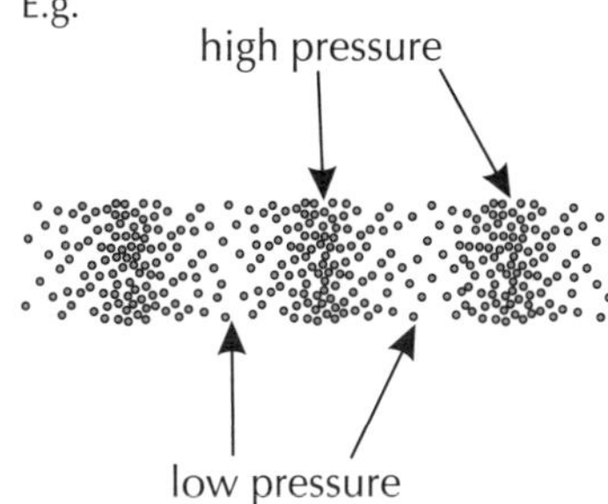

b) A wave with repeating patterns of high pressure and low pressure.

c)

d) It moves back and forth around a fixed point.

2 a) sound, frequency / pitch, hear

b) E.g. ultrasound can travel through objects to clean places that couldn't be reached by hand.

c) The higher frequencies of ultrasound means it vibrates the dirt more.

3 Microphones convert sound waves to electrical signals, whereas loudspeakers do the opposite and convert electrical signals into sound waves.

4 a) particles, back, forth, vibrating, high pressure, low pressure

b) An ultrasound wave causes particles in the body to vibrate. These vibrating particles hit other particles and transfer energy to them, causing them to move. The wave is passed on in this way until energy is transferred to the particles in the deep tissue.

c) Ultrasound will travel quicker through solids and liquids since the particles within a solid or liquid are closer together than in a gas. A pressure wave travels by particles hitting each other. This process is faster when the particles are closer together.

Topic 7 — Separating Mixtures

Page 40 — Before you Start

1

Pure Substance	Mixture
nitrogen gas diamond	fruit juice milk seawater air

2 The boxes ticked should be "A pure substance has a fixed melting point" and "Melting and boiling points can be used to help identify pure substances".

3 a) Evaporation b) Condensation
c) Evaporation d) Condensation
e) Condensation

Page 41 — Filtration and Evaporation

1 Filtration separates **insoluble** solid substances from a liquid. A mixture of flour and water can be separated using filter paper. The water particles are small enough to pass through the filter paper — the water is called the **filtrate**. The flour particles are too big to pass through the filter paper so they stay behind — this flour is called the **residue**.

2 a) True

b) False
The amount of matter always stays the same, even if it is in a form that you cannot see.

c) True

d) True

3 a) E.g. the pebbles are a lot bigger than the sand particles, so he could separate the pebbles from the sand using a sieve.

b) The sand particles cannot pass through the filter paper so stay behind, whereas the seawater can pass through because the particles are smaller.
Residue: sand. Filtrate: seawater.

c) The water in the seawater evaporates as it has a relatively low boiling point. The salt/dissolved substances in the water will be left behind.

Pages 42-43 — Chromatography

1

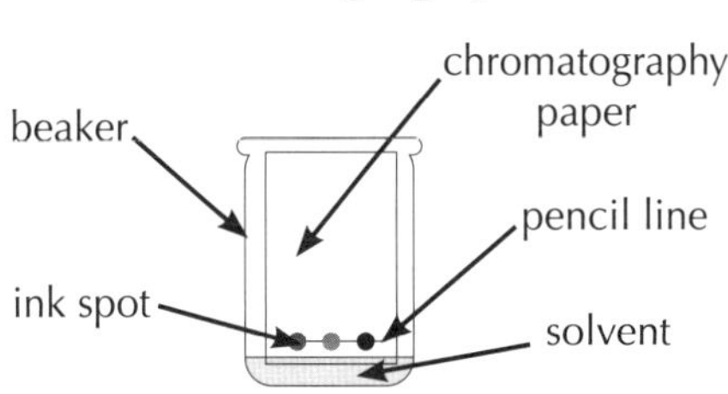

2 a) No, some travel further than others.

b) i) She is correct. There are multiple substances because there are multiple spots. One of the spots is at the same height as substance A, so it could contain the same substance.

ii) She is incorrect. An insoluble substance would not move at all.

c) There is only one spot for substance A, so it could be formed by just one substance. However, it could be that multiple substances all travel the same distance to produce one spot.

3 a) i) From these results, it looks like there are at least three different substances between the four samples.

ii) The paint from shirt 1 can be ruled out as it has an additional substance present that isn't in the paint from the message.

b) It can't be the paint from shirt 3 as it does not have the new substance shown in the sample from the wall. It could still be the paint from shirt 2 as it does have the new substance.

c) The substances in the ink in a pen can be separated by the solvent as well. Pencil marks are not moved by the solvent.

Pages 44-46 — Distillation

1 a) Evaporation/boiling and condensation.

b) They must have different boiling points.

2

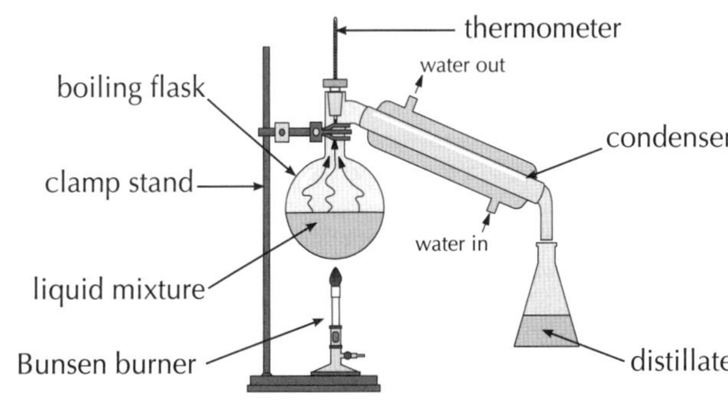

3 Correct order: 2, 4, 1, 5, 3

4 a) The first liquid will have the lowest boiling point, but water has the highest boiling point (100 °C).

b) Liquids A and B will evaporate off at a lower temperature and leave the water behind.

c) Liquid A and liquid B have very similar boiling points. This means that it will be very difficult to control the temperature to allow liquid A to evaporate off without liquid B evaporating too.

Answers

d) i) At 65 °C, the water is still a liquid. Liquid A would be boiling, and liquid B would be close to boiling.
ii) At the top of the column, the temperature is cool enough to cause the substances to condense. This means they do not flow down the condenser, but back down the fractionating column.

5 a) Adding more water will mean that the oil is able to float on top more easily, and the sand will sink to the bottom.
b) i) Fraction 2 will be water.
ii) Kerosene and diesel may overlap slightly as their boiling point ranges are close together (they meet at 250 °C).
iii) He is correct that it has a very high boiling point as the substance did not evaporate when the diesel came off the column at a temperature of around 350 °C. He is incorrect as it is not necessarily a pure substance, but could be a mixture.

Topic 8 — Reactions with Acids and Alkalis

Page 47 — Before you Start

1 a) Indigestion tablet: alkaline
b) Tomato juice: acidic
c) Pure water: neutral
d) Stomach acid: acidic
e) Bleach: alkaline

2 pH, green, Acids, red, Alkalis, purple

3 The reversible changes are:
Melting butter in a pan
Freezing water in an ice cube tray
Boiling water in a kettle

Page 48 — Chemical Reactions

1 a) True
b) False
Physical changes can usually be reversed easily as the particles have not been rearranged like in a chemical reaction.

2 a) magnesium + sulfur → magnesium sulfide
b) calcium carbonate → calcium oxide + carbon dioxide
c) zinc + lead nitrate → zinc nitrate + lead

3 a) This is a chemical reaction because a new substance is formed.
b) Dissolving is a physical change because no new substance is formed.

Pages 49-51 — Neutralisation Reactions

1 An alkali is an example of **a soluble** base.
A base is a substance that neutralises an **acid**.
Neutralisation reactions form a salt and **water**.

2 Hydrochloric acid: potassium chloride
Sulfuric acid: copper sulfate
Nitric acid: sodium nitrate
Citric acid: aluminium citrate

3 a) Neutralisation reactions always form a salt. If the salt is soluble, you won't be able to see it because it will be dissolved in the water.
b) Lithium chloride
The first part of the name of the salt comes from the lithium hydroxide, and the second part comes from the hydrochloric acid.
c) E.g. She could use universal indicator, which would turn green when the solution is neutral.
d) The lithium hydroxide will increase the pH and can make the acid less harmful/corrosive.

4 a) An antacid is a base/alkali that neutralises the acid, making the acid less acidic (raising the pH). This helps to relieve the heartburn as there is less acid present/the acid concentration is reduced.
b) Too many antacids may make the enzymes involved in food digestion less effective as there may be less stomach acid present/the acid concentration is reduced.
c) Aluminium chloride
d) i) Magnesium chloride
ii) The production of bubbles of carbon dioxide gas causes fizzing.
iii) The antacid with magnesium carbonate is more likely to cause this side effect because it forms a gas (carbon dioxide) during the neutralisation reaction. This gas is released into the stomach, where the reaction takes place.

5 a) Potatoes and strawberries
b) i) pH 6.5–7.0
ii) The calcium carbonate reacts with the acids in the soil to neutralise them. This raises the soil pH.

6 a) Zinc oxide neutralises the acid in the bee sting so that it is less acidic.
b) Zinc oxide is a base so it cannot neutralise another base. You should use an acid instead, e.g. vinegar, to neutralise the alkaline sting.
There are lots of other substances in stings that also cause pain — not just the acids or alkalis.

Topic 9 — Reactions with Metals and Non-Metals

Page 52 — Before you Start

1 The metals are: gold, mercury, titanium, silver, iron.

2 An acid has a pH of below 7.
An alkali is a soluble base.

3

Physical Change	Chemical Reaction
sugar dissolving in water	iron turning into rust
seawater evaporating to leave salt	wood burning on a bonfire
ink spreading out in water	vinegar fizzing with baking soda

4 zinc + sulfur → zinc sulfide
You could also have written zinc and sulfur the other way round.

Page 53 — Oxidation of Metals and Non-Metals

1 a) False
Oxidation reactions are when substances combine with oxygen.
b) True
c) False
Non-metal oxides are usually acids, which can neutralise bases.

2 a) lithium + oxygen → lithium oxide
b) More than 7
Metal oxides are bases so when they dissolve in water their pH must be above 7.

3 a) potassium
b) i) Both iron and copper can be oxidised and change colour. Only iron oxide is called rust — copper oxide is not rust.
ii) It takes a lot longer for iron oxide (rust) and copper oxide to form than for potassium and lithium to oxidise.

Page 54 — Metals and Acids

1 a) A metal-acid reaction will produce bubbles because the reaction forms a gas.
b) Hydrogen
c) i) calcium sulfate ii) lead nitrate

2 a) i) magnesium ii) gold
b) Zinc is more reactive because the bubbling gets faster during the reaction, whereas in the reaction of tin the bubbling stays slow.
c) magnesium + nitric acid → magnesium nitrate + hydrogen

Pages 55-56 — Displacement Reactions

1 more, less, most reactive

2 a) copper

Answers

b) Iron sulfate has been produced in the reaction. Iron sulfate solution is green rather than blue like the copper sulfate solution.

c) iron + copper sulfate → copper + iron sulfate

3 a) E.g. sodium azide breaks down at a lower temperature than potassium azide, so the reaction occurs more easily/ can be started more quickly.

b) E.g. the potassium metal produced in the reaction would be highly reactive and therefore more dangerous.

c) sodium + iron oxide → iron + sodium oxide

4 a) i) The magnesium is able to displace/take the place of the copper in the copper sulfate.

ii) magnesium + copper sulfate → copper + magnesium sulfate

b) He could try to react copper with zinc sulfate — if he is right, no reaction will happen. Or he could try to react zinc with copper sulfate — if he is right, a reaction will take place.

c) Reactivity series from most reactive to least reactive: magnesium, zinc, lead, copper.

d) He should react copper with silver nitrate solution — if the teacher is right, the copper will displace the silver as it is more reactive.

Pages 57-61 — The Reactivity Series and Extraction

1 chemical, more, substances

2 a) yes b) no c) yes d) no e) no

3 a) The substance between potassium and calcium would have a very violent reaction (as it is near the top of the reactivity series and is therefore very reactive). The substance between zinc and copper would have a much slower reaction with the acid (as it is less reactive).

b) Reactivity series from most reactive to least reactive: potassium, **Y**, calcium, magnesium, zinc, **X**, copper.
Y must be more reactive than X, because Y reacts with water but X doesn't. This means it must be higher up the reactivity series.

c) Both metals X and Y are above copper in the reactivity series/are more reactive than copper, so will be able to displace the copper in the copper chloride solution.

4 a) i) copper oxide + **carbon** → **copper** + carbon dioxide

ii) **iron oxide** + **carbon** → iron + **carbon dioxide**

b) Aluminium is more reactive than carbon, so carbon cannot be used to displace the aluminium in aluminium oxide.
Carbon can only be used to extract metals that are below it in the reactivity series.

5 a) From most reactive to least reactive: calcium, iron, silver

b) yes
Iron is more reactive than silver, so it will displace the silver in the silver nitrate solution.

c) Iron is less reactive than calcium so cannot displace the calcium from the calcium chloride.

d) Calcium is more reactive than iron, so will displace the iron in the iron sulfate to form calcium sulfate and iron.

6 a) Lead is more reactive than copper so the lead would displace the copper in the copper nitrate to form lead nitrate and copper.

b) i) Tinplate is a better substance to use because it is less reactive and won't react with the drink, even if it gets hot/ it is used for hot drinks.

ii) The aluminium oxide protects the aluminium underneath, by stopping substances that might react with the aluminium from touching it.

iii) Tin can be extracted with carbon because it is less reactive than carbon. Aluminium can't be extracted with carbon as it is more reactive than carbon. So pure aluminium was not available until other methods of extracting it were invented.

c) iron + oxygen → iron oxide
zinc + oxygen → zinc oxide

7 a) calcium

b) cobalt + oxygen → cobalt oxide

c) E.g. gold is not very reactive so it will not react with the oxygen or water in air.

d) Reactivity series from most to least reactive: calcium, cobalt, copper, silver, gold.

e) The copper is more reactive than the silver. It can react with the gases in the air to form the green substance, which can stain the skin.

8 a) Reactivity series from most to least reactive: barium, manganese, nickel, mercury, gold.
E.g. barium must be more reactive than manganese as it oxidises more quickly in air. Manganese is more reactive than nickel as manganese reacts with steam but nickel does not. Both manganese and nickel are more reactive than mercury, as mercury doesn't react with hydrochloric acid. Mercury is more reactive than gold because it doesn't exist as a pure metal and it has to be extracted.

b) Between manganese and barium.

Topic 10 — The Universe

Page 62 — Before you Start

1 True, False, False, True

2

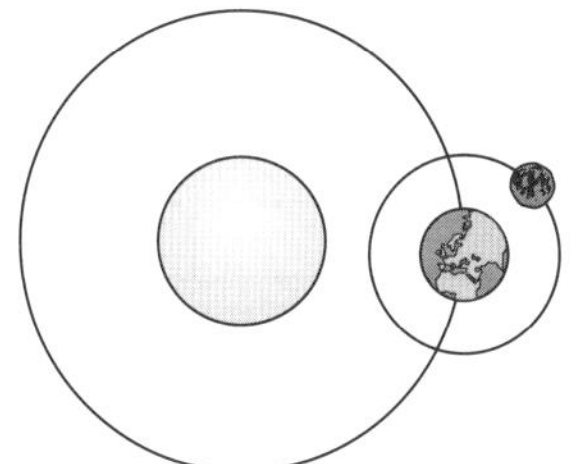

The Moon orbits around the Earth, and the Earth orbits around the Sun.

3 The Moon is a rocky **sphere** that orbits the **Earth**.
It is a natural **satellite**.
The Moon's orbit takes about a **month**.
The Moon is bright because it **reflects** light.

Pages 63-65— The Solar System

1

Venus
Jupiter
Neptune
Asteroids
Sun
Earth
Saturn
Mercury
Mars
Uranus

2 a) B
A is wrong because Y is to the left and Z is to the right — Nicolaus will be able to see Z on the left and Y on the right. C and D are wrong because Nicolaus won't be able to see planet W.

b) The planets reflect light from the Sun, which then travels back to Nicolaus so he can see them.

c) A planet that orbits a star outside of our solar system.
Nicolaus wouldn't be able to see those planets — they'll be much too far away and not bright enough to be visible to the naked eye. He might see the stars that they orbit around though.

3 a) The Sun and the planets appear to move across the sky (and the Earth doesn't feel like it is moving) so it is easy to believe the Sun and the planets orbit around the Earth.

b) E.g. If the planets orbited the Earth, they would always move across the sky in the same direction, before coming around again.

Answers

4 a)

Summer Winter

Sun

b) Summer

c) The tilt of the Earth's axis means that the UK is tilted towards the Sun in summer so it spends longer in sunlight. In the winter the UK is tilted away from the Sun so it spends a shorter time in sunlight.

d) It stays almost the same.
Places near the equator don't change how far they are away from the Sun much, so day length doesn't change much either.

e) The tilt of Earth's axis means that in winter in the UK the sunlight generally arrives at a shallower angle, so the same energy is spread over a larger surface area. In the summer, the light is focused on a smaller area and more energy is transferred.

5 a)

Planet	Gravitational strength (N/kg)	Ziggog's weight (N)
Hecate	2	150
Singe	17.1	**1282.5**
Turtle	5	**375**
Osiris	6.9	**517.5**
Elatha	22.5	**1687.5**

b) i) Hecate and Turtle
ii) Hecate

c) Elatha probably has the largest mass. Gravitational strength increases with mass, so the planet with the largest mass will be the one with the strongest gravity.

d) Ziggog is wrong — the gravitational force is higher between objects that are closer together, so it will be stronger between Osiris and Rha.

Pages 66-67 — Stars and Galaxies and the Universe

1 a) E.g. A star is a body in space that gives out its own light.
Some of the things we can see in the night sky are visible because they reflect light, like the Moon and planets.

b) E.g. A galaxy is a group of lots of stars that are kept together by gravity.

c) E.g. The Milky Way is the name of our galaxy.

2 a) i) The distance that light travels in one year.
ii) The numbers would be too big if we used km.
In light years, the numbers are smaller so are easier to handle.
In fact, 1 light year is about 9 461 000 000 000 km.

b) i) 1.3 light seconds.
ii) 1.3 light seconds = 380 000 km.
So the light second is bigger.

c) 8 light minutes.

3 a) We see Proxima Centauri as it was 4.2 years ago.

b) i) 4.2 light years × 18 500 years/light year
= **77 700 years**
ii) E.g. It would take much longer than one human lifetime to travel, so spacecraft would have to be big enough to have a lot of humans who can reproduce on the way there.

c) i) E.g. The further away a star is, the older the light is that reaches Earth. So looking at distant stars lets us look into the past.
ii) The star would be so far away that the first light it gave out won't have reached us yet.

Topic 11 — Movement

Page 68 — Before you Start

1 fish and frog
Slugs and jellyfish don't have skeletons — they use fluid in their bodies to keep their shape and move around.

2 toenails and tongue

3 a) No b) Yes c) Yes
d) No e) Yes

4 Bones work together with **muscles** to make the body move. For this movement to happen, **a force** must be applied to the skeleton.

Pages 69-70 — The Skeletal System

1 a) ligament
b) tendon

2 a) Any one from: e.g.

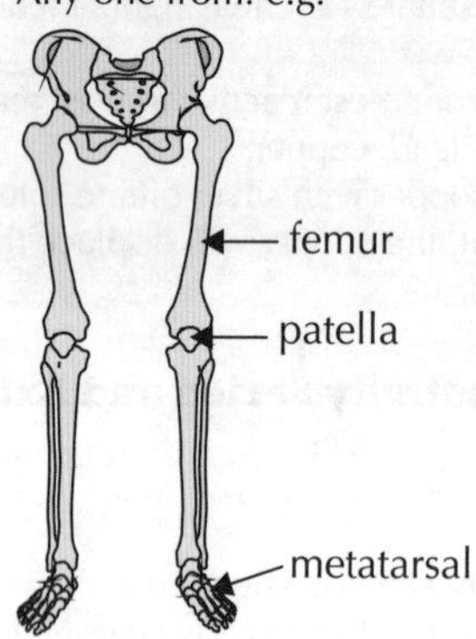

b) It allows the leg to move.

c) i) E.g. uterus/womb / bladder / small/large intestine
ii) E.g. bone has a strong outer layer that is rigid and tough. This means it can stop any impact to the body from damaging delicate organs.

3 a) e.g. hard outer layer and soft centre

b) i) bone marrow
ii) It produces red and white blood cells.

4 a) E.g. the tent poles share the function of support. Just as the skeleton provides a rigid frame for the rest of the body to hang off, the tent poles provide a rigid frame for the material of the tent to hang off. This allows the tent to stand up. / The tent poles share the function of protection. Just as the skeleton is rigid and tough to protect delicate organs inside, the tent poles are rigid and tough and provide a strong frame to protect the contents inside.

b) E.g. I partly agree with Leo because the tent poles and the skeleton share the same functions of support and protection. However, the tent poles do not share any other functions of the skeleton. They do not help the tent to move or produce blood cells.

5 E.g.

Function	Why has it been affected?	How might this affect day-to-day life?
Support	The bones in his legs are softer than they should be, meaning they're also likely to be weaker and so less able to support the weight of his upper body.	Frank's leg bones may be painful. / He may not be able to stand for long periods of time.
Movement	The cartilage at his knee joints has been broken down, meaning there's less material there to reduce friction where his two leg bones meet.	Frank may struggle to bend his knees. / He may experience pain when he walks.

Answers

Pages 71-72 — The Muscular System

1 **a)** relaxation/contraction, relaxation/contraction, movement, contracts
b) E.g. the small intestine, where muscle helps to move food along to the large intestine.

2 **a)** tendon
b) A pair of muscles that work against each other, to move a bone at a joint.
c) When the triceps contracts and the biceps relaxes, the ulna (and the radius) are pulled down by the triceps. When the biceps contracts and the triceps relaxes, the radius (and the ulna) are pulled up by the biceps.

3 **a)** (13.0 + 30.3 + 32.5 + 40.7 + 22.6 + 29.5) ÷ 6
= **28.1 s**
b) The time the person could keep the weight in position.
c) i) e.g. the weight and the biceps
ii) e.g. a newton meter
d) E.g. this may not be true for all masses or weights. / She only looked at a very small sample of people / She did not repeat the experiment and take an average of several tries.
e) E.g. a heavier weight would have meant that the biceps muscle had to exert a bigger force on the arm bone to hold it up. Some of the friends' biceps may not have been strong enough to do this.

Topic 12 — Digestion

Page 73 — Before you Start

1 People need to eat the right types of food.

2 A — 3, B — 2, C — 4, D — 1

3 stomach — churns food to help break it down
large intestine — absorbs water into the body
mouth — tears food into bits for swallowing
small intestine — absorbs nutrients into the blood

Pages 74-75 — Nutrition

1 **a)** butter, nuts, milk
b) They are used as a source of energy.

2 dehydration, small, fibre, complex

3 **a)** A diet that contains all of the right components in the right amounts.
b) Iron is important for red blood cells.
c) Cow's milk is a good source of calcium, which is important for strong bones and teeth. If people don't drink cow's milk they may not get enough calcium in their diet, so having it in soya milk helps these people to stay healthy.

4 **a) i)** Carbohydrates are the body's main source of energy.
ii) Yes, because e.g. wholemeal toast contains complex carbohydrates and jam contains simple carbohydrates.
b) i) protein
ii) Protein is important for building new tissue / for growth and repair.
iii) Any two from: carbohydrates / fibre / vitamins / minerals
c) i) Fibre helps food move through the digestive system, so not enough fibre could mean it's difficult to eliminate waste, which leads to constipation.
ii) E.g. yes, because fibre is contained in foods such as fruits and vegetables and she doesn't eat many of these.

Pages 76-77 — Diet

1 **a)** Daily BER = 5.4 × 24 × 57 = **7387.2 kJ/day**
b) Energy required for running = 2900 × 1.5 hrs
= 4350 kJ
Total energy required = 7387.2 + 4350
= **11 737.2 kJ/day**

2 **a)** 10 500 ÷ 100 × 20 = **2100 kJ**
b) E.g. he could be more likely to get infections. / He could get a deficiency disease.
c) Any two from: e.g. nuts / beans / seeds.
d) scurvy and iron deficiency anaemia
Scurvy is caused by a lack of vitamin C. Iron deficiency anaemia is caused by a lack of iron.

3 **a)** If you take in more energy from your diet than you use up, your body stores the extra energy as fat. This causes weight gain. If a person weighs over 20% more than is recommended for their height they are classed as obese.
b) E.g. high blood pressure and heart disease.
c) E.g. losing weight could help obese people become healthier, as they would be less likely to get associated problems such as high blood pressure and heart disease. However, to be healthy people need to eat a balanced diet. Replacing some meals with only fruit and vegetables may lead to an unbalanced diet as the person may not be getting enough of some nutrients, such as fat and protein. The person may also not be getting a full range of vitamins and minerals and may develop deficiency diseases, such as iron deficiency anaemia.

Pages 78-80 — The Digestive System

1 The molecules contained in food are too big to be absorbed by the body. The digestive system breaks the big food molecules down into smaller ones, which can be absorbed from the digestive system into the blood. The small molecules can then be carried to cells, where they are taken up for use in life processes.

2 **a)** Water is absorbed into the blood.
b) It helps to churn the contents of the stomach. This helps to break down the food and means it gets mixed with digestive juices, which speeds up digestion.
c) i) E.g. without a stomach, she doesn't have a sac in which a large meal can be stored before it enters the intestines.
ii) Digestion starts in the mouth with chewing. This starts the mechanical breakdown of food. Also, saliva in the mouth contains enzymes, which starts the chemical breakdown of some food molecules/carbohydrates.
iii) The food will enter the large intestine. Here, water from the food will be absorbed into the blood and the remaining food matter will become faeces. The faeces will then enter the rectum where they will be stored until they are eliminated from the body, via the anus.

3 **a)** E.g. bacteria that are naturally present in our bodies don't make us ill. Also, the bacteria that help in digestion aren't found in the stomach, they're found in the intestines.
b) E.g. bacteria produce enzymes that aid digestion. / Bacteria help us digest food that we couldn't digest otherwise, such as plant cells.

4 **a)** Enzymes speed up the chemical reactions of digestion, which helps break down food faster.
b) i) It means that food molecules can be absorbed into the blood easily and transported away to the other body cells.
ii) If the villi are flattened, there is less surface area for absorption. This will decrease the number of molecules that can be absorbed at the same time and so may mean the person doesn't absorb enough nutrients before the food moves out of the small intestine.

5 **a)** The amylase has broken down the starch molecules into smaller sugar molecules, which can pass through the holes in the Visking tubing into the water.
b) Any two from: e.g. it shows large molecules being broken down into smaller molecules. / It shows how enzymes in the small intestine help digestion. / It shows how small molecules can pass through a membrane with small holes in it.
c) Any two from: e.g. concentration of starch solution / volume of starch solution / volume of amylase solution / temperature of water / temperature of starch solution / temperature of amylase solution / time waited for (30 min)

Answers

Topic 13 — Plant Reproduction

Page 81 — Before you Start

1 Something that contains seeds.
2 a) reproduction
b) adaptation
c) Dispersal
d) pollination
3 Examples of pollination:
A bee transferring pollen between flowers.
The wind blowing pollen grains out of cherry blossom.
Examples of seed dispersal:
A conker dropping from a tree and rolling away.
A bird eating a cherry.
A dog getting seeds stuck on its coat.
The wind blowing a dandelion 'clock'.

Pages 82-83 — Pollination and Fertilisation

1 a)

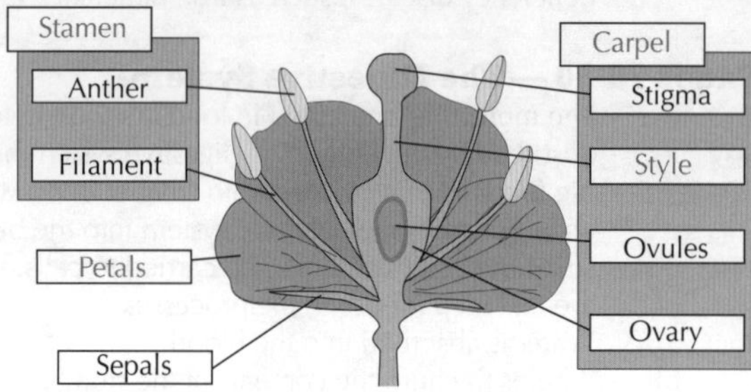

b) E.g. to support the stigma.
c) in the ovary
d) The sepals need to be tough to protect the flower in the bud. The petals don't need to be as tough for their function of attracting insects.
e) If the stigma has a sticky surface, pollen is more likely to stick to it so pollination is more likely.
2 male, anthers, stigma, ovule
3 a) True
b) False
The joining of a nucleus from a male and female sex cell is called fertilisation.
c) True
4 a) In self-pollination pollen is transferred to the female part/stigma of the flower on the same plant, whereas in cross-pollination the pollen is transferred to the female part/stigma of the flower on another plant.
b) It will mean self-pollination is less likely and will encourage cross-pollination. This will benefit the plant because too much self-pollination can be a disadvantage.
c) To increase the chance that they do get pollinated, because having the stigma and anthers closer together will encourage self-pollination. Self-pollination is better than no pollination.

Page 84 — Types of Pollination

1 a) E.g. it might have colourful petals to attract insects.
b) i) No. It is a flower because it contains the plant's reproductive organs.
ii) E.g. wind-pollinated because it has long filaments that hang the anthers outside the flower so pollen can be easily blown away.
iii) Lighter pollen is more easily carried by the wind so it will be more likely to reach other plants.
2 a) To stop selected plants from being wind-pollinated by plants that haven't been selected for breeding.
b) E.g. Hena could use a paintbrush to take pollen from the anthers of selected wheat plants and brush them onto the stigmas of other selected wheat plants.

Pages 85-86 — Seeds

1 a) The structure that contains the embryo of a plant. It develops from the ovule.
b)

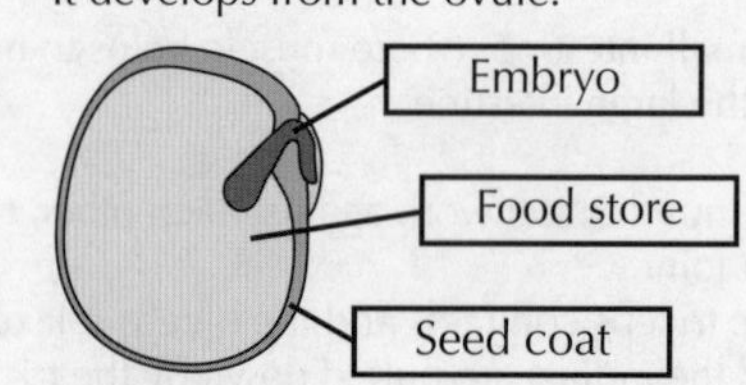

c) the ovary
2 a) Attaching to his fur means that the seeds are dispersed (carried away from the parent plant and other seeds), so that when they drop off and start to grow they will have less competition for resources like space, light, water and minerals.
b) E.g. they have spikes/hooks to stick to animal fur.
c) E.g. animals can eat seeds and then move to a different area. When the seeds come out in the animals' droppings, they will be far away from the parent plant.
d) Animals getting pollen on their fur is part of pollination, whereas what happened to Graham is part of seed dispersal.
3 a) <u>Model 3</u>
$20 + 27 + 22 = 69$
$69 \div 3 =$ **23 cm**
<u>Model 4</u>
$38 + 34 + 30 = 102$
$102 \div 3 =$ **34 cm**
<u>Model 5</u>
$27 + 28 + 26 = 81$
$81 \div 3 =$ **27 cm**
b) E.g. Lee could be right because the mass of the models will affect how fast they fall and so should be controlled. Model 5 could have been a lot heavier than the other models, making it fall faster and closer to the drop point.

Topic 14 — Human Reproduction

Page 87 — Before you Start

1 To create sex cells and protect the foetus.
2 True, False, True
3 B
The human egg is one of the biggest cells in the human body — about 0.1 mm across. Sperm are really small compared to the egg — the head is about 0.004 mm long.
4 A child inherits characteristics from both their mother and their father.

Pages 88-89 — Human Reproductive System

1 a) Fertilisation happens inside the fallopian tube/oviduct.
b) In a pregnant woman, the baby develops inside the uterus.
c) Sex cells are called gametes.
2 a)

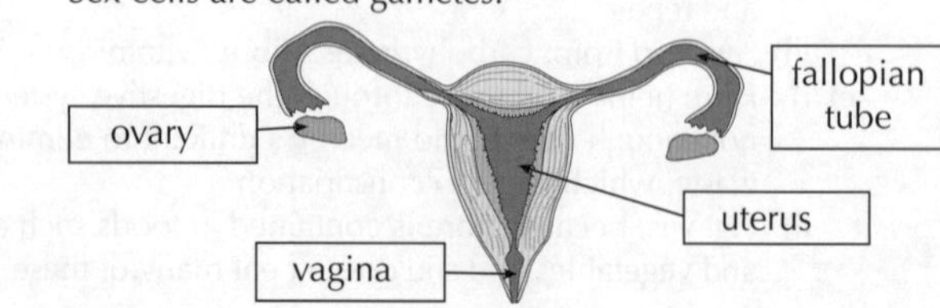

b) i) ovaries
ii) ovulation
iii) fallopian tube, uterus
c) the vagina
3 a) i) The testis/testes/testicles
ii) The testes produce and store sperm.
b) i) the penis
ii) It swells/stiffens.
iii) It leaves the body.

Answers

c) i) It stops / sperm can't be transported out of the testicles any more.

ii) If the sperm can't leave the male body/ reproductive system, they won't be able to enter a female reproductive system and fertilise an egg.

Page 90 — The Menstrual Cycle

1 a) Stage 1 — The lining of the uterus breaks down and passes out of the vagina — the woman has a period.
Stage 2 — The lining of the uterus starts to build up.
Stage 3 — An egg is released from one of the ovaries.
Stage 4 — The lining of the uterus stays thick in case an egg is fertilised.

b) 28 days
Remember, this is an average for the menstrual cycle — the length of a cycle can vary a lot between different people.

c) i) During stage 3 / after day 14.

ii) Because fertilisation is most likely to happen when the egg has been released from the ovaries, whilst it is still in the oviducts/fallopian tubes.

iii) Just after a woman's period / stage 2.
This is because the egg and the lining of the uterus should have passed out of the woman's body, so the egg can't be fertilised. However, there is no time in a woman's menstrual cycle where it's certain she can't get pregnant.

d) i) The cycle stops (and menstruation usually stops).

ii) An embryo/foetus.

2 No ovulation means no egg is released. If no egg is released, it can't get fertilised by a sperm.

Pages 91-93 — Fertilisation and Development

1 nuclei, oviducts/fallopian tubes, uterus, implants, gestation

2 a) i) F ii) D iii) A
iv) C v) E vi) B

b) i) It contracts to push the baby out.

ii) They expand so that there is room for the baby to pass through.

3 a) Mother to foetus: nutrients.
Foetus to mother: carbon dioxide, waste products.

b) umbilical cord

c) Liquid: amniotic fluid. Function: it protects the foetus from bumps/knocks/if the mother falls.

d) The baby can't breathe because it is surrounded by amniotic fluid not air.

4 a) The egg won't be able to travel down the fallopian tube and sperm won't be able to swim up it. So the egg won't get fertilised.

b) The sperm won't be able to travel through the female reproductive system to meet the egg and so the egg won't be fertilised.

5 a) Going into labour/giving birth before the baby is fully developed.

b) i) Irene: 2 × 75 mg = **150 mg**
Alex: 100 mg + (2 × 80 mg) = **260 mg**

ii) Alex

c) E.g. to avoid harming pregnant women and their babies.

Topic 15 — Evolution

Page 94 — Before you Start

1 inherited
environmental
both
Having big muscles is a mixture of inherited features (like how easily you can build muscles) and environmental effects (like how much exercise you do to build muscles).

2 You should have ticked B and D.
A is false because evolution will have happened over this time period (two million years), so species will have changed. Some species will also have gone extinct.
C is false because there is variation within a species.

3 a) E.g.

Hawk
Blackbird
Caterpillar
Rabbit
Grass

b) grass

c) blackbird and hawk

d) e.g. caterpillar and rabbit

Pages 95-96 — Natural Selection

1 variation, competing, reproduce, offspring, genes, adapted, extinct

2 a) E.g. when two or more organisms want the same resource and have to struggle against each other to get it.

b) i) beak length

ii) Birds with longer beaks will be able to reach nectar in the flowers better.

3 a)

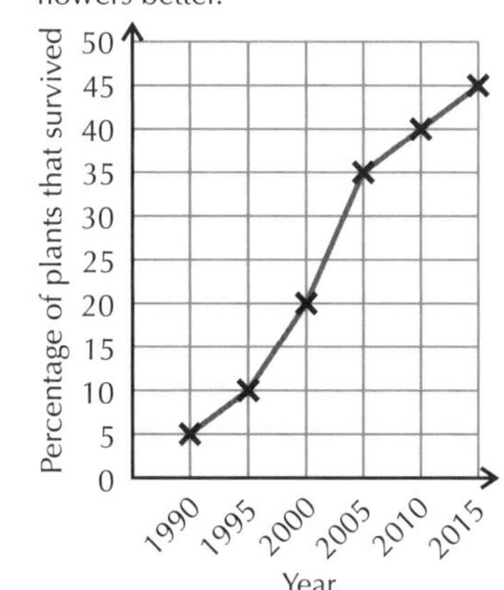

b) The percentage of plants that survived in soil that contained metals increased from 1990 to 2015.

c) That the percentage of plants that survived had increased again.

d) E.g. because it shows that individuals that survive are passing their characteristics/genes on to their offspring, so their offspring can also survive in contaminated soil/when the soil contains metal.

e) E.g. it went extinct because no new plants could grow from the seeds.

Page 97 — Theory of Evolution

1 a) E.g. the idea that organisms present today have developed from species that existed in the past.

b) E.g. natural selection means that species adapt to their environment, so over long periods of time this can cause a whole species to change and so evolve.

c) E.g. no — evolution occurs as species become adapted to their environment (through natural selection), so there is no purpose and no perfect organism.

2 a) E.g. the shell could have evolved from the ribs. They could have flattened even more than the ones in *E. africanus* and joined/fused together to form a solid shell.

Answers

b) E.g. shells provide protection from predators, so the Chelonians with shells would have been more likely to survive and reproduce than ones without shells. So Chelonians with shells would have been more likely to pass their genes/characteristics on to their offspring and shells would have evolved in the species by natural selection.

Pages 98-99 — Biodiversity

1 a) i) E.g. that there are a lot of different types of organism/species living in the rainforest.
ii) E.g a group of organisms of the same species in one area.
b) E.g. food / medicine.
c) i) To store the hereditary material/genes of different species.
ii) Because organisms are interdependent — animals and plants will rely on trees for things like food and shelter, in order to survive.
iii) Because there's likely to be more variation between organisms in larger populations. So, if the environment changes, there's likely to be more organisms that have the characteristics/genes they need to survive and reproduce.

2 a) i) 10 species
Make sure you read the graph three years after the starfish were removed, not at year 3 itself, i.e. year 2 + 3 years = year 5.
ii) $((5 - 17) \div 17) \times 100 = (-12 \div 17) \times 100$
$= -70.58... = $ **-70.6%**
This shows that the number of starfish has decreased by 70.6% from when they were removed to 10 years after the experiment started.
b) i) it increased
ii) The populations of other species will have decreased because a greater number of mussels will have been able to compete more successfully with other species for space and food. This means that some of the other species will have struggled to survive.
c) E.g. it means that the scientists can see if they get the same results in other places / if there are differences in the results.

Mixed Questions

Pages 100-104

1 a) E.g. because chromatography separates mixtures of dissolved (coloured) substances ***[1 mark]***.
b) water ***[1 mark]***
c) 2 ***[1 mark]***
Dye number 2 was not carried up the chromatography paper so must not have dissolved in the solvent. This means it's not soluble in the solvent.
d) 1 ***[1 mark]***

2 a) Any two from: change direction / change shape / rotate/turn. ***[1 mark for each correct answer]***
b) it's stationary ***[1 mark]***
it's travelling at a constant speed ***[1 mark]***
c) E.g. the ground is causing a force that pushes up on Dev ***[1 mark]***. This force is equal and opposite to the force caused by gravity pulling him down, so they're balanced ***[1 mark]***.

3 a) i) 2 A ***[1 mark]***
There are twice as many cells so the current is doubled.
ii) 1 A ***[1 mark]***
Circuit 3 is the same as Circuit 1, but the ammeter is in a different position — this will have no effect on the ammeter reading.
b)

Ammeter	Current (A)
A_1	**3.0**
A_2	**1.0**

[1 mark for each correct answer]
Remember, the total current remains the same but splits up along the branches of a parallel circuit.

4 a) i) Stage Two ***[1 mark]***
ii) Because a low level of Hormone A means that the uterus lining might not thicken as well ***[1 mark]***, which means the embryo might not be able to implant/embed into the lining and develop ***[1 mark]***.
b) i) menstruation ***[1 mark]***
ii) So that the embryo isn't lost from her body ***[1 mark]*** and the lining of the uterus is preserved for it to develop in ***[1 mark]***.
c) The alcohol could pass from Danni's blood to the foetus' blood through the placenta ***[1 mark]***.

5 a) hamstring ***[1 mark]***
b) i) The ball will drop ***[1 mark]*** because if the quadriceps relaxes, the hamstring will contract ***[1 mark]***, to pull the lower leg downwards ***[1 mark]***.
ii) The ball will drop ***[1 mark]***.
If the calf muscle contracts it will pull the heel back and cause the toes to point.

6 a) potassium hydroxide and sulfuric acid ***[1 mark]***
b) magnesium chloride ***[1 mark]***, hydrogen ***[1 mark]***

7 a) Refraction: **B** / **E** ***[1 mark]***
Reflection: **C** ***[1 mark]***
b) it slows down ***[1 mark]***
it bends towards the normal ***[1 mark]***
c) When white light hits a raindrop it gets dispersed/split up ***[1 mark]***, so that it shows the full rainbow/spectrum of colours ***[1 mark]***.
d) Blue ***[1 mark]***. The blue filter would absorb every other colour except blue, so that only blue passed through it ***[1 mark]***.

S8W32